SPOOKED

SPOOKED

How the CIA Manipulates the Media and Hoodwinks Hollywood

NICHOLAS SCHOU

FOREWORD BY DAVID TALBOT

Hot Books

Hot Books may be purchased in bulk at special discounts for sales promotion, corporate gifts, fund-raising, or educational purposes. Special editions can also be created to specifications. For details, contact the Special Sales Department, Skyhorse Publishing, 307 West 36th Street, 11th Floor, New York, NY 10018 or info@skyhorsepublishing. com.

Hot Books® and Skyhorse Publishing® are registered trademarks of Skyhorse Publishing, Inc.®, a Delaware corporation.

Visit our website at www.skyhorsepublishing.com.

10 9 8 7 6 5 4 3 2 1

Library of Congress Cataloging-in-Publication Data is available on file.

Cover design by Brian Peterson

Print ISBN: 978-1-5107-0336-0
Ebook ISBN: 978-1-5107-0341-4

Printed in the United States of America

For Charles Bowden and Gary Webb

"All governments are run by liars, and nothing they say should be believed."
—I.F. Stone

Foreword

Y ou're holding in your hands the latest Hot Book, one in a series of compact, deeply researched, and highly provocative books on the most burning topics of our day. As the editorial director of Hot Books, and as a journalist and historian who has scrutinized the shadowy operations of our national security state, I view *Spooked* as a particularly timely and urgent exposé of power. As whistle-blowers such as Edward Snowden have made clear: power prefers to operate in the dark. And national security elites—especially in the United States, where we have witnessed the growth of a permanent war state and an enormous empire of surveillance—do everything they can to cloak their activities in secrecy.

Now more than ever, we need a robust and aggressive press to report on this increasingly secretive national security state, and the military operations (and criminal actions) that are often carried out in our name. American freedom begins with freedom of the press. Without an informed citizenry, there can be no democracy. But unfortunately, as *Spooked* shockingly documents, our media is too often an accomplice of our national security agencies, rather than our guardians of freedom.

The CIA's long, cozy relationship with the media dates back to the Cold War, when our great press watchdogs obediently trailed the heels of spymaster Allen Dulles as the agency wreaked havoc on democratic governments and sovereign nations around the world and even subverted democracy at home. When Dulles and his agents overthrew Iran's prime minister Mohammad Mossadegh on August 19, 1953 (a tragedy that still has no end), the *Washington Post* editorial board saw the calamity as "a cause to rejoice." The CIA's criminality put the *New York Times* in a similar celebratory mood, with its editorialists condemning the fallen Mossadegh as "a rabid, self-seeking nationalist." In reality, the deposed prime minister was simply a reform leader who believed that his country's oil resources should be owned by the people of Iran rather than by Western energy giants. The *Times* told its readers that Mossadegh's violent overthrow "brings us hope." Instead, what it brought was decades of tyranny and sorrow, and the continuing hatred and enmity of Iran against "The Great Satan."

Likewise, the following year, when the CIA cooked up a military coup against Guatemala's president Jacobo Arbenz, the *New York Times* was once again all too willing to do the spy agency's bidding. Arbenz was a progressive reformer who, like Mossadegh, had antagonized corporate clients of the Dulles brothers—in this case the all-powerful United Fruit Company—by redistributing some of its vast holdings to the country's miserably poor peasant farmers. But according to the CIA's spin artists, Arbenz was a dangerous

Communist who was giving the Soviet empire a foothold in our hemisphere. When the reporting of *Times* foreign correspondent Sydney Gruson seemed to contradict this CIA narrative, Dulles simply expressed his concerns to his old friend *New York Times* publisher Arthur Hays Sulzberger, and the problem—i.e., the insufficiently compliant Gruson— disappeared. He was kept safely away from Guatemala as the CIA went about its dark mischief. In the future, Sulzberger assured the CIA spymaster, the newspaper's coverage of Guatemala would be screened "with a great deal of more care than usual."

The correspondence files of the late Allen Dulles, stored in a Princeton library, are stuffed full of chummy letters between the godfather of US intelligence and many of America's top media executives, editors, reporters, and broadcasters. The casual and convivial mind meld between US intelligence and the media establishment is on full display in this voluminous correspondence. Dulles and the journalists, whose job it was to monitor his shadowy agency, sipped cocktails and rubbed elbows at prestigious organizations such as the Council on Foreign Relations in New York, at Washington power dens such as the Alibi and Metropolitan clubs (two of Dulles's favorite watering holes), and at the Georgetown townhouses of CIA-friendly pundits such as Joe Alsop.

This unseemly collusion was finally exposed by Carl Bernstein in a 1977 *Rolling Stone* article, penned eight years after Dulles's death. The piece was explosive, revealing that more than four hundred journalists had carried out secret assignments for the CIA over the previous twenty-five years, including some who were on the agency's payroll. Washington was shocked, *shocked* by Bernstein's exposé, and the CIA duly promised to conduct its relations with the press in a more professional and transparent manner.

But, as Nicholas Schou reveals in *Spooked*, if the CIA is now more careful about how it goes about manipulating the media, its influence, if anything, is more pervasive these days and no less pernicious. CIA officials might no longer ply journalists with liquor and slip them cash as was common in the past, but they do dole out favors that are no less essential to a national security reporter's career: the tips and leaks from a secretive bureaucracy without which the news stories begin to dry up. In today's downsized media business, top Washington news slots are extremely competitive positions. Thus ambitious journalists soon learn to play ball with the right people at CIA headquarters in Langley, Virginia, if they value their professional future.

Despite the reluctance of most journalists and former CIA officials to break ranks and talk openly about the "spooking of the press," Schou succeeds in cracking this code of silence. From the Cold War to the War on Terror, he shows us how the Langley media machine works. *Spooked* provides the kind of revelations and insights that the press, loath to report on its own failings and corruptions, seldom supplies. Schou alerts us to the vital stories that get covered up, the courageous journalists who get punished, and the disastrous national security decisions made when the press becomes too complicit with those in power.

As the manipulation of America's free press becomes more deeply institutionalized, fact-based reality turns into an increasingly ephemeral concept. The world of make-believe is taking over, filling the vacuum left by our weakened media, with more and more people getting so-called news from entertainment sources. Recognizing the growing power of Hollywood to shape the public's perception of reality, the CIA also makes a strong effort to influence the movies and TV shows with national security themes as they move along the creative assembly lines. *Spooked* chronicles how the producers, directors, writers and stars of movies such as *Zero Dark Thirty* and *Argo* and TV shows such as *Homeland,* are all too happy to give CIA personnel supervisory powers and screen credits in return for the dubious benefits of private tours of CIA headquarters and meetings with CIA bigwigs. Meanwhile, films and TV series that challenge the CIA's paranoid worldview and expose the crimes of the US national security state rarely get made and when they do, are indifferently marketed and quickly disappear.

Spooked is that rare work of journalism that rips through the curtain behind which our most secretive agencies operate. It will no doubt outrage and infuriate readers as they discover the many ways they have been deceived and misled by those whose job it is to enlighten us. Hopefully, it will also compel readers to demand that our watchdogs in the press and public office do much more to monitor the national security state that is steadily overshadowing our democracy.

Our body politic has grown sluggish and dull-witted, stuffed with a steady diet of junk media and corporate propaganda. It's time to light a fire under this slumbering giant: American democracy. It's time to think dangerous thoughts. Welcome to Hot Books.

—David Talbot, editorial director of Hot Books/Skyhorse and author of the *New York Times* bestseller *The Devil's Chessboard: Allen Dulles, the CIA, and the Rise of America's Secret Government*

Contents

Introduction

T he CIA has a long history of "spooking the news," dating back to its earliest days when legendary spymaster Allen Dulles and his top staff drank and dined regularly with the press elite of New York and Washington—including the top executives and editors of the *New York Times, Washington Post, Time, Newsweek,* and CBS—and the agency boasted hundreds of US and foreign journalists as paid and unpaid assets. In 1977, after this systematic media manipulation was publicly exposed by congressional investigations, the CIA created an Office of Public Affairs that was tasked with guiding press coverage of intelligence matters in a more transparent fashion. The agency insists that it no longer maintains a stable of friendly American journalists, and that its efforts to influence the press are much more above board. But, in truth, the US intelligence empire's efforts to manufacture the truth and mold public opinion are more vast and varied than ever before.

During a recent interview at CIA headquarters in Langley, Virginia, a pair of CIA public affairs officers confirmed they provide journalists with frequent background briefings, typically about foreign hot spots. Their mission, they stated, is simply to guide news coverage of national security issues in a truthful direction, while also protecting personnel and operations from public disclosure. "Our role at the Office of Public Affairs is not to manipulate reporters," one CIA spokesperson told me. "If they come to us with questions about nonclassified information that makes us look bad, we just give our typical comment."

The CIA has a longstanding tradition of providing briefings to favored journalists, he acknowledged. "In the 1980s, Bob Woodward came out here a lot of times to get briefed," the press officer said, referring to the *Washington Post* reporter of Watergate fame. But the agency is happy to speak with any journalist seeking its perspective on global crises. "Now, we get a lot of calls about the crisis in the Middle East. Reporters want a basic understanding of what's happening."

This all sounds reassuring and harmless. But the reality is, beneath the new professionalism that supposedly characterizes today's relationship between the CIA and the press lurks a vast underworld of covert pressure, seduction, and deception aimed at controlling media coverage of the most vital national security issues. Since 9/11, the national security establishment has ballooned to encompass thousands of government agencies and private contractors. Although the CIA retains a central role in this sprawling labyrinth, it by no means is the only covert institution that seeks to impose Washington's view of the world on the public at large, by working the levers of what Cold War–era CIA wizard Frank Wisner called the agency's "mighty Wurlitzer," on which he could play any propaganda tune.

After WikiLeaks burst onto the scene and whistle-blowers Chelsea Manning and Edward Snowden rocked the national security world, it seemed like a new day of transparency might be dawning. But instead of emboldening the media to more aggressively cover the vital issues of war and peace, and surveillance and freedom, national security reporters were subjected to tightening controls and increased intimidation.

For every editor who defies the national security establishment, or maverick blogger who embarrasses the CIA or National Security Agency (NSA), there are numerous cases of editorial compliance. The notion that, in the age of Snowden, the American press has become a sharp-eyed watchdog of the growing security state is far-fetched. In truth, the Washington press corps continues to largely function as a mouthpiece for the government when it comes to covering the endless war on terror.

This deference to the national security state has a long history. The collaboration between the CIA and the press began with the birth of the agency in 1947. The Vietnam War and Watergate scandal briefly strained this compact. But, with the Reagan counterrevolution in the 1980s, the media came under powerful new pressures to conform to the official line. Even as the CIA waged a secret and illegal war in Nicaragua, and US-backed military regimes in Central America massacred innocent civilians, reporters who went too far in exposing these crimes and atrocities were subjected to intimidation and smear campaigns by Reagan officials and their allies in the corporate media. Independent-minded correspondents were reassigned; careers were destroyed.

In the early 1990s, during the Persian Gulf War, the US news media all too willingly embedded itself within the US military, temporarily attaching itself as a communications branch of the government and demonstrating that the Vietnam-era days of critical war reporting were over. Following the September 11, 2001, terrorist attacks, the shift became permanent when the press—led by the *New York Times* and *Washington Post*—turned itself into a propaganda tool of the US government, spreading Bush administration lies about Saddam Hussein's nonexistent weapons of mass destruction program, and paving the way for America's 2003 invasion of Iraq, whose disastrous consequences continue to haunt us.

This book explores how the US media got "spooked" by the CIA and other powerful agencies of the national security state. *Spooked* features firsthand accounts from prominent national security reporters as well as former CIA officers, who speak for the first time about how the spy agency tries to spin press coverage of everything from its controversial drone assassination program to the agency's deliberate disinformation campaign about Iraqi WMDs.

Spooked also sheds new light on the CIA's increasingly cozy relationship with Hollywood. The agency has established a very active spin machine in the heart of the entertainment capital, which works strenuously to make sure the cloak and dagger world is presented in heroic terms. Since the mid-1990s, but especially after 9/11, American screenwriters, directors, and producers have traded positive portrayal of the spy profession in film or television projects for special access and favors at CIA headquarters.

According to former CIA officers whose exploits have been depicted onscreen, as well as ex-spooks who currently consult with Hollywood, the spy agency allows filming inside its headquarters and often extends red-carpet treatment to directors and stars of CIA-friendly projects like *24*, *Argo*, *Homeland*, and *Zero Dark Thirty*, with the latter screen drama particularly exemplifying the agency's deep grip on popular culture. Although Hollywood's depiction of the CIA has shifted back and forth between the light and dark over the decades, with the 1970s being a low point for the agency's portrayal on screen (*The Parallax View, Three Days of the Condor*), more recent films and TV programs demonstrate that the entertainment industry has become much more enthralled by the intelligence community.

In a democratic society, there is always a struggle between the machinery of national security and press freedom, and the public's right to know is usually the loser. When our national security czars become, in effect, our media gatekeepers, we lose one of the essential cornerstones of a true democracy—an informed citizenry. Distracted by the manufactured flow of information produced by a news media that has fallen under the spell of its own official sources, and beguiled by militaristic and patriotic Hollywood mythmaking, the American public is largely benighted when it comes to understanding the wars and covert violence carried out in our name. *Spooked* will explain exactly how this process occurs and what happens to journalists who dare to break the rules.

The increasingly sophisticated ability of intelligence agencies to manipulate reality has enormous consequences for our democracy. After fifteen years of never-ending press accounts about terror threats and Islamic bogeymen, a paranoid reality reinforced by even more breathless Hollywood thrillers, the American people have become all too willing to give up their freedoms and acquiesce to a state of permanent war.

James Risen of the *New York Times* is one of the few mainstream reporters who has been willing to challenge the enormous power of the national security state, much to his own personal and professional peril. He has learned firsthand that this empire of secrecy always wants to "control the press and limit what you write."

"If you go beyond those limits, you will be punished," says Risen. "We have built a national security state worth billions of dollars that is trampling our civil liberties and we are living with a fear of threats that are not there."

Chapter One

"I Eat Pretty Much Anything"

O n December 23, 2013, in response to a pair of Freedom of Information Act (FOIA) requests, the Central Intelligence Agency released 574 pages of emails between various national security reporters and the agency's public affairs office. The massive trove of material remained out of the public eye for a year, but in late 2014, it finally surfaced in a series of articles published by the online investigative magazine, the *Intercept*. The articles landed like a bombshell, revealing how some of America's most prominent national security reporters were functioning essentially as unpaid CIA assets, sending the agency detailed story notes and, in at least one case, entire drafts of articles prior to publication.

Roughly half of the released emails concerned just one reporter, Siobhan Gorman, who recently left the *Wall Street Journal* for a better paying job with Brunswick, a privately held global communications company. Her email communications with the agency revealed her interest in touring the agency's Langley headquarters, writing a story about its gym, and securing a personal meeting with then-agency director, David Petraeus, who the CIA confirmed to Gorman was fond of running six-minute-miles during work breaks and would give face-to-face interviews to any reporter who could run a mile in under seven minutes.

In March 2012, Gorman accepted the CIA's invitation to an "off-the-record dinner" with Petraeus. "Great! Do you have any food allergies?" an agency public affairs officer replied. "Nope," Gorman confided, "I eat pretty much any-thing." (Petraeus ultimately lost his job after sharing classified information with his biographer, mistress, and fellow work-out fanatic, Paula Broadwell, who authored a book based on her special-access relationship with the general appropriately titled *All In*.)

In a separate exchange of emails that month between Gorman and a CIA press officer, whose name was redacted by the agency, she passed along a tip from a "colleague" at the *Wall Street Journal* who had told her that he had heard a rumor that there had been an assassination attempt against President Hafez al-Assad of Syria. "Happy Sunday! A col-league heard that Assad has been shot," begins Gorman's cheerful note. "Sounds unlikely, but it's a crazy time. Any truth to that?" Promising to look into the rumor, Gorman's agency contact inquired if her colleague was in Syria. "No," Gorman responded, continuing in the same share-too-much-informa-tion vein. "This colleague is actually the editor of the paper."

In a subsequent email, Gorman thanked the press offi-cer for his help. "As I mentioned, tips from our editor don't always pan out but we have to check because it's from our editor and he claims to talk frequently to people in MI-6," she explained, referring to the British intelligence agency. A few months later, on May 1, Gorman sent the CIA an email titled "Translating the UBL Trove" in which she asked for an update on the agency's efforts to pull useful intelligence from Osama bin Laden's computer files, which had been seized exactly a year earlier, during the raid on his Pakistani compound in which the world's most wanted man was killed. "Hi guys, so do I wish you a happy anniversary today?" she asked, sounding just like one of the gang at Langley.

The CIA's response to that email (along with nearly every other one in the entire file) was completely redacted, presumably not to protect US national security (because why would the agency be divulging top secret information in emails to reporters?) but more likely because of the embarrassing light they shed on the incestuous relationship between journalists and the agency's PR department. Yet even the less damaging material that somehow made it past CIA censors reveals the extent to which, far from acting like a watchdog protecting the public from government excesses, the US national security press has almost completely fallen under the spell of the powerful intelligence complex it purports to monitor.

Langley's press relations officers, who asked to remain anonymous, claim their job is more difficult now than ever, especially in the current media landscape where anyone with a computer can post potentially damaging information online that can quickly be picked up by a succession of blogs or websites before exploding on social media platforms like Twitter. The media terrain is indeed more challenging for the intelligence community since 2013, when former National Security Agency (NSA) contractor Edward Snowden began leaking a stream of top-secret files on the NSA's massive surveillance operations directed against American citizens, and even friendly governments. The Snowden revelations, along with the earlier WikiLeaks release of shocking documents and videos related to America's post 9/11 wars obtained from army whistle-blower Bradley (now Chelsea) Manning, shifted the ground under the espionage empire's feet.

These days, security officials sometimes feel they are playing catch-up with a new world of anonymous hackers and independent bloggers. "Since Snowden, we are unsuccessful ninety percent of the time," one CIA spokesperson glumly estimated, in reference to his efforts to convince reporters to either kill a story or delay it, at least long enough for the agency to protect its undercover assets and operations—or to protect Langley's ass. "The hard part for us is we can't comment, so we have to do this weird Kabuki dance and say, 'If you publish this story, this is what will happen.' I don't have any control over the media," he insisted. "All I can do is to make a case not to publish the story, but usually we are unsuccessful because sensitive information has already been leaked."

The *Intercept,* which the CIA spokesperson specifically cited as an example of a hostile media outlet, has published a string of embarrassing stories about the CIA's recent excesses in the past few years. The most notable was "The Drone Papers," based on leaked paperwork supplied by a high-level intelligence source showing that far more innocent civilians than suspected militants have been killed by US remote-controlled air strikes, in fact by a stunning ratio of six to one. More alarming (to the CIA, at least) than the leaked documents themselves is the fact that the leaker is apparently someone other than Edward Snowden, who earlier had provided one of the *Intercept*'s founding editors, Glenn Greenwald, a former blogger for the *Guardian* and *Salon*, with reams of classified NSA material. (The *Intercept's* other founding editors are Laura Poitras—the second person Snowden approached, and whose documentary *Citizenfour* chronicled Greenwald's meeting with Snowden in

Hong Kong—and Jeremy Scahill, the best-selling author of the books *Blackwater* and *Dirty Wars*.)

Then there's the online magazine *VICE News*, which employs one of the most aggressive and intrepid national security reporters in the business, Jason Leopold, whom the FBI has dubbed a "FOIA terrorist" for his extensive use of the Freedom of Information Act to gain access to government documents. Leopold, who lives in Los Angeles, is a rare example of a national security reporter who doesn't work in Washington, D.C. "There's a reason for that," he said in a recent interview just days after returning from Capitol Hill, where he testified to Congress about how US intelligence agencies have deliberately stymied his Freedom of Information Act efforts at extracting government information in the public interest. Living outside the Beltway, conceded Leopold, limited his "immediate access—but that means I become much more aggressive in terms of trying to get information, and I don't fall victim to 'access journalism.' Being in D.C. just for a week, I mean you can get completely swallowed by this bureaucracy and become chummy-chummy with people, whereas I want to keep that distance."

Bryan Bender, *Politico*'s defense editor, who has covered the national security beat from within Washington, D.C., for more than a decade, agreed with that assessment. "If you are a journalist covering the national security state, there is often a price for access," Bender acknowledged. "You don't just call up the CIA and say, 'I am doing a story; please answer my questions.' If you are lucky, they will be helpful. But if they are going to be helpful, it's usually because they have already decided that you're a good reporter and you're going to be fair to them."

* * *

Despite the CIA's complaints about a news pack that has supposedly become more snarling since Snowden, most reporters working the national security beat are still happy to play by the agency's rules, which includes giving Langley's public affairs office at least a day's notice of an impending story. The Washington press extends the same courtesy to allied intelligence agencies. One example involves the publication of the identity of "Jihadi John," the Islamic State terrorist responsible for several beheadings of hostages, including reporters James Foley and Steven Sotloff, and aid workers David Haines, Alan Henning, and Peter Kassig. As first reported by *Washington Post* reporter Adam Goldman, the masked executioner was actually a Kuwaiti-born British national named Mohammed Emwazi. (Emwazi was killed by an American drone strike in Raqqa, Syria, in late 2015.) When Goldman informed British intelligence he was going to publish Emwazi's name, officials asked him to hold off for twenty-four hours.

Although they didn't explain the reason, in this case it turned out to be valid. "I didn't know that at the time, but they needed to get his family out of England [to Kuwait] so they wouldn't be lynched," Goldman recalled. "We always take the government's case seriously. Sometimes they make legitimate cases and we listen. There's this idea we always poke them in the eye, but we have relationships. Sometimes you don't know everything; you have only a sliver of it. You've gotten a piece of it but don't know the whole story."

This is a favorite tactic of the CIA when trying to kill a story it doesn't want published: to claim that the story will endanger the lives of its employees or others. As with the Jihadi John case involving British intelligence, sometimes these CIA requests to hold off on a story are clearly legitimate, but often they are much murkier. In 2012, for example, two CIA employees driving in a car with diplomatic plates were ambushed on a road just outside Mexico City by out-of-uniform Mexican federal police who were likely working with a drug cartel. The officers only escaped alive because of very skilled defensive driving by one of them. When the story broke, it was revealed that US officials were attacked, but their agency was not identified. British journalist Ioan Grillo, who was working for a major wire service at the time (which he prefers not to name), said he called the head of the DEA in Mexico, who told him that the Americans weren't his people.

"The fact that the US embassy was not identifying them made it smell fishy right away," Grillo said. "I called a former head of international operations for the DEA and he revealed the truth, that they were CIA." When Grillo told his editors, they had their CIA reporter contact Langley. The CIA replied with an aggressive email, in which it tacitly admitted they were agency employees but urged the wire service not to publish that information because, as the attack demonstrated, lives were in danger. "Senior editors at the news agency were cowed right away, and actually asked [me] if their agency affiliation was important," Grillo recalled. "We ended up sitting on the story. Within a day, a Mexican newspaper revealed they were CIA, likely from a leak in the Mexican government. I was frustrated at losing the scoop, and how the news agency had been cowed so easily. In a story like this, the CIA was never going to be able to keep it under wraps."

Indeed, given the highly competitive reporting climate when it comes to covering the CIA, there are perils to holding off on a story for too long, something that *Newsweek*'s Jeff Stein learned when he discovered who really assassinated Imad Mugniyah, the Hezbollah terrorist "mastermind" who died in a mysterious February 2008 car bombing in Damascus, Syria. Few Americans had even heard of Osama bin Laden when Mugniyah began sowing terrorism in Lebanon and elsewhere. He was thought to be responsible for the 1983 bombing of the US embassy and Marine barracks in Beirut, as well as the kidnapping and murder of CIA near east director Robert Ames. Mugniyah was also suspected of orchestrating the 1982 bombing of the Israeli embassy in Buenos Aires, as well as a Jewish community center a few years later.

Although his 2008 demise—the result of a textbook-perfect, targeted assassination that killed only Mugniyah—had long been reported as the work of the Mossad, Israel's intelligence agency, Stein discovered that it was, in fact, a CIA hit personally approved by President George W. Bush. After he pulled together the final details of the operation in fall 2013, Stein wanted more than a routine "no comment" from the CIA, he wanted its cooperation. And the veteran national security reporter thought he would get it, because his scoop seemed to show the agency at its best—taking out a dangerous terrorist with a long rap sheet of murder and mayhem to his name. "If ever you could justify a retaliatory kill, this was it," Stein recalled telling agency officials. "And this bomb was shaped in a way that there could be no collateral damage, no other civilians, no family, nobody else would be killed. I knew that the techies were sent back again and again to develop a shaped charge that would only get Mugniyah. That was my pitch: it was a clean, justifiable kill."

But to Stein's surprise, the CIA responded by insisting that publishing the piece would place overseas agents at risk of execution by Hezbollah, the Islamist militant group based in Lebanon. *Newsweek's* editor in chief, Jim Impoco, agreed to hold the story at Langley's request, and then sat on it. Months passed, then a year. "Sometimes you withhold a story because it doesn't serve any purpose to publish it and you could get somebody killed," Stein acknowledged. "But they *always* say that you're going to get people killed." In a November 2013 meeting at CIA headquarters, top agency officials made a "forceful case" for spiking the story altogether. "In the geopolitical context at that moment, the CIA made a very persuasive case," Impoco said.

Finally, on the evening of Friday, Jan. 30, 2015—more than a year after Stein turned in his article about Mugniyah's assassination—he got a call from an agitated agency official tipping him off that the *Washington Post* had the story and was going with it, despite CIA pleas not to publish. Stein replied that *Newsweek* would certainly publish too. The official then went back to the *Post* and informed its reporters that he'd told *Newsweek* about its plans. The *Post* decided to rush the story, which had been scheduled for the Sunday paper, onto its web page. Around 10:00 p.m. that Friday, the story, cowritten by Adam Goldman and Ellen Nakashima, exploded online. Stein had been scooped.

There were significant differences in their stories: the *Post's* story reported Israelis had coordinated and carried out the hit for the CIA from a control room in Tel Aviv. Both Goldman and Stein stand by their versions. "I had three impeccable sources that the Israelis pulled the trigger," says Goldman.

"Tel Aviv was too distant for an operation that required split-second timing," Stein countered. "The whole point was that the Israelis had presented the CIA with Mugniyah's location in Damascus so that the agency could personally retaliate against him for the murder of so many Americans. It was like a friendly deal between mobsters—something right out of *The Sopranos*." But in any case, it was no longer Stein's exclusive story.

Does he regret that his editors sat on the story at Langley's request? "Yes and no," Stein said. "I did agree that the CIA had a strong case for not publishing when we first went to them in October 2013. Hezbollah had militant factions that would see the CIA as bragging and agitate for a response. A year later, however, with Hezbollah firmly part of Lebanon's government, and with the rise of ISIS resulting in a de facto alliance between [Hezbollah] and the CIA in Syria, I thought the situation had changed and we could publish. But it wasn't my call."

* * *

Adam Goldman of the *Post* has a history of breaking news much more quickly than not only his rival reporters but also the CIA itself might prefer. Most recently, in January 2016, Goldman and fellow *Post* reporter Greg Miller broke a story about an internal CIA practice known as an "eye-wash," by which the agency circulates two separate and contradictory memorandums regarding sensitive operations, with the accurate memo being kept in a much tighter circle, thus effectively deceiving the agency's own employees—and demonstrating the lengths to which the CIA will go with its disinformation campaigns. Senate investigators looking into the agency's torture of detainees had uncovered the practice, finding numerous examples where the CIA internally falsified reports about drone strikes and other operations around the world.

In 2012, Goldman, then an Associated Press reporter, and his colleague, Matt Apuzzo, now with the *New York Times*, got wind of a bombing plot by al-Qaeda in the Arabian Peninsula timed to take place on May 1, the first anniversary of Osama bin Laden's death. The plot involved planting a bomb on a transatlantic passenger jet bound for the United States. Under pressure from both the White House and the

CIA, the AP agreed to hold the story for a week, because, as Goldman later wrote, a "sensitive intelligence operation was still under way." However, after learning from his sources that the government planned to make the bomb plot public, the AP published the story a day before President Obama formally announced the news. The story led to the Justice Department's seizure of the AP's telephone records involving Goldman, Apuzzo, and their sources.

In Goldman's view, being first to the story sometimes involves pissing off powerful people. "First of all, I'm not an access journalist," he explained. "They don't get real stories; they get shit. You need to know you'll lose sources, and that's okay; you'll make new ones. For a lot of people, that's their worst fucking fear. But if you're not losing sources you're probably not doing your job."

While at the AP, Goldman and Apuzzo also scooped the *New York Times* on a story that the newspaper had sat on for six years involving Robert Levinson, a US citizen who had disappeared on an island off the coast of Iran in 2007. After Levinson's disappearance, government sources told reporters that he was a private investigator looking into cigarette smuggling. But this cover story fell apart when *Times* reporter Barry Meier interviewed a lawyer for the family, who gave him access to Levinson's files in return for a promise not to publish anything that would jeopardize his safety. The paperwork proved that the CIA had actually hired Levinson to spy on Iran. Meanwhile, the AP's Goldman and Apuzzo also learned of Levinson's CIA ties. After holding onto the story for three years, the wire service finally published it on December 13, 2013, despite appeals by both the White House and Senator Bill Nelson (representing Levinson's home state of Florida) not to do so. By acting more obediently to government wishes, the *Times* lost its hot exclusive.

In an official statement, Katherine Carroll, AP's executive editor, strongly defended her call: "In the absence of any solid information about Levinson's whereabouts, it has been impossible to judge whether publication would put him at risk. It is almost certain that his captors already know about the CIA connection but without knowing exactly who the captors are, it is difficult to know whether publication of Levinson's CIA mission would make a difference to them. That does not mean there is no risk. But with no more leads to follow, we have concluded that the importance of the story justifies publication." Previously, Terry Anderson, an AP editor who was kidnapped in Beirut by Hezbollah in 1986 before being released five years later, had been the longest-held American hostage in US history. As of the writing of this book, Levinson, who remains missing, holds that record.

Overall, Adam Goldman's assessment is correct. Those national security reporters who push against or defy the intelligence establishment's rules of the game wind up with the best scoops. But it takes courage to do this. Those who reject access journalism and break away from Langley's embrace are violating a long tradition of media cooperation with the national security state.

Chapter Two

For God and Country

In 1977, former *Washington Post* reporter Carl Bernstein published a stunning exposé of the Central Intelligence Agency's tentacle-like stranglehold over the news media. The story ran twenty-five thousand words and named numerous prominent media executives and reporters who had worked closely with the CIA (and in some cases were on the agency payroll) during the previous three decades. This enlistment of US journalists was in direct violation of the CIA's charter, which forbids spy operations and propaganda directed at the American public. The CIA, Bernstein reported, had viewed the recruitment of journalists as "among the most productive means of intelligence gathering employed by the CIA."

Because of the corporate media's longtime collaboration with the CIA, which dated back to the agency's inception in 1947, it took three decades before a maverick journalist like Bernstein could pierce the wall of silence and break the explosive story. And when Bernstein did break the story, he didn't do it in the *Washington Post*, the newspaper where he had become famous for his Pulitzer Prize–winning coverage of the Watergate scandal. He published it in *Rolling Stone* magazine, the countercultural voice of his generation.

Tellingly, Bernstein gave his own former newspaper— one of the principal media partners of the CIA—a pass in the *Rolling Stone* exposé. Nonetheless, the prominent CIA media assets that Bernstein did name—including Time Inc. founder Henry Luce, CBS chairman William Paley, and *New York Times* publisher Arthur Hays Sulzberger—were enough to rock the Fourth Estate. The top executives and editors at these media giants often formed tight bonds with CIA big-wigs like Allen Dulles and Richard Helms, allowing their reporters to serve as agency informants and sometimes giving spies a media cover for overseas operations.

According to Bernstein, the CIA "cut back sharply" on the practice of directly employing American journalists at home and overseas after 1973. But while the agency no longer covertly employs or *directly* controls the work of American reporters, foreign journalists are another matter.

"There was really a break period in the CIA's relationship with the press from 1973 to 1976," recalled Frank Snepp, a former CIA officer in Vietnam who spent years briefing the press. CIA director William Colby, who took over the CIA following the Watergate scandal, began backing away from recruiting reporters as assets. Later, CIA chief George H. W. Bush made it official. "He said no more hiring of journalists, they will not be paid assets," according to Snepp. "But what was the caveat? We didn't rule out foreign journalists."

The London press, long under the influence of British intelligences services, was particularly vulnerable to manipulation by US spy agencies. "As a CIA agent, I fed information to reporters who fed it to *The Economist*," Snepp said. "I actually wrote pieces that made it into *The Economist*. I'm not saying *The Economist* was a CIA dupe, but they were an outlet of choice for the things we wrote."

In 1973, James Schlesinger, who had replaced Richard Helms as CIA director earlier in the year, ordered his officers to compile a list of all the agency's illegal activities, a nearly seven hundred–page report that came to be known as the CIA's "Family Jewels." The most shocking revelations in the report concerned the CIA's assassination plots against foreign leaders, including Cuba's Fidel Castro (which proved unsuccessful) and Congo's Patrice Lumumba, which resulted in the charismatic African leader's brutal murder. Less remembered are the disclosures about the CIA spying on American journalists and activists.

In 1971, for instance, CIA Director Helms ordered the surveillance of *Washington Post* reporter Michael Getler. "In addition to physical surveillance, an observation post was maintained in the Statler Hilton Hotel where observation could be maintained of the building housing his office," the report stated. "The surveillance was designed to determine Getler's sources of classified information of interest to the agency which had appeared in a number of his columns." Similarly, between February and April 1972, the CIA used its Hilton Hotel spy nest to snoop on muckraking columnist Jack Anderson and his "leg men" Brit Hume (now a *Fox News* political analyst), Leslie Whitten, and Joseph Spear. "The purpose of this surveillance was to attempt to determine Anderson's sources for the highly classified agency information appearing in his syndicated columns."

Even as he ordered these illegal operations, Helms lied to his own officers about what they were reading in the press. "I gave a talk to the American Society of Newspaper Editors last winter, as you know, and I did it for only one purpose. That was to try and put in the record a few of these denials that we've all wanted to see put in the public record for some time," Helms said in a September 17, 1971, "State of the Agency" speech to CIA employees. "And you can rely on those denials. They're true, and you can use that as any text that you may need to demonstrate that we're not in the drug traffic, and that we're not trying to do espionage on American citizens in the United States, and we're not tapping telephone lines, and that we're not doing a lot of other things which we're accused of doing. . . . I would like to suggest that if you have it in your hearts to do so that you speak up when the occasion arises and try and set the facts straight."

Former Saigon station chief William Colby, who succeeded Schlesinger as CIA director in 1973, heeded Helms' call when he sent a letter to *Parade* magazine editor Lloyd Shearer, denying that the CIA's biggest intelligence-gathering effort of the Vietnam War, Phoenix Program, was an "assassination" program. "Thank you for your kind and informative letter of January 11 concerning Phoenix Program," a good-natured Shearer responded. "I don't want to get into a running word-battle with you on the subject of political assassination in Indo-China or the role of the CIA and other of our agencies in Phoenix Program," he wrote. "I am just wondering if you would care to say flatly that the CIA has never used political assassination in Indo-China or elsewhere and has never induced, employed, or suggested to others that such tactics or devices be employed. If you will make that flat statement under oath, I will not only apologize, I will tango with Dick Helms in [department store] Garfinkel's largest show window at Fourteenth and F—providing, of course, Mrs. Helms gives her permission."

Colby gamely took the challenge. "I can say, under oath if need be, that CIA has never carried out a political assassination, nor has it induced, employed, or suggested one which occurred," he told Shearer. "Whether this fully meets your challenge, I cannot say (it takes two to tango)."

The back-and-forth session seems to have ended there, with a copy of Colby's response preserved in the Family Jewels file accompanied by a note from then-CIA public affairs director Angus Thuermer, who advised Colby, "I suggest we let the whole thing drop." This was wise advice, because in truth, the CIA's Phoenix program *was* an assassination and torture program, claiming the lives of over twenty-six thousand suspected Viet Cong officials and agents, among whom were a significant number of innocent civilians.

* * *

CIA veteran Frank Snepp, who spent five years in Vietnam briefing reporters and interrogating high-level Phoenix Program prisoners, was one of the last agency employees to leave the country in April 1975, just as the Family Jewels scandal was coming to light. Few people were as deeply involved in the CIA's manipulation of the media during the war as Snepp. "This is how disinformation worked," Snepp recently explained. "Say we're in a dry-season infiltration period, which would be the fall of any year. We would tell the press that sixty-thousand enemy troops had just entered South Vietnam from the Laotian border, and that we required additional aid from Congress. What we didn't give them were estimates of recent enemy casualties on the border, which also numbered sixty-thousand. We said the whole North Vietnamese Army was moving into the war zone when, in fact, they were simply making up for casualties. But if you admitted that, it was impossible to persuade Congress every year to vote for additional aid. Unless the press is able to deconstruct that half-truth, they are going to think the communists are sending hordes south and we will have South Vietnam overrun unless Congress gives additional aid. That's what I was ordered to do."

According to Snepp, the CIA favored certain journalists, but felt no need to hire them, while others were secretly working on behalf of the agency. "There were journalists who were almost, if not completely, CIA assets, as opposed to agents of influence, people we could expect a friendly response from," he said.

One example of the former was the legendary syndicated columnist Joseph Alsop, whose Georgetown house was a watering hole for spooks, politicos, and the media elite. As Bernstein revealed in his 1977 *Rolling Stone* exposé, Alsop wasn't just friendly to the agency, he was actually on its payroll. When confronted with his CIA complicity, Alsop told Bernstein he was proud of it, seeing it as his patriotic duty: "The notion that a newspaperman doesn't have a duty to his country is perfect balls."

In either 1969 or 1970, Snepp said that Alsop arrived in Saigon to get a briefing, staying at the US ambassador's house. The CIA's Saigon station chief, Ted Shackley, instructed Snepp to brief Alsop in person. When Snepp arrived at the residence that evening, Alsop greeted him in a lady's evening gown. As it turned out, Snepp was the only CIA officer in Saigon who didn't already know that Alsop was a closeted homosexual and occasional cross-dresser. He was also a Langley favorite, who was regularly given access to inside information, as Snepp soon found out. As the young press handler began feeding Alsop the agency's latest propaganda points about the war, Alsop sharply corrected him with the actual facts, which were still classified. "The evening rapidly deteriorated and I had to run out of this guy's place, with Marine guards snapping to attention as I went," Snepp recalled with a laugh. "I went back to the CIA headquarters and everybody, including Shackley, thought this was the funniest thing they'd ever seen." Shackley told Snepp that the CIA had long pandered to Alsop because he was such a reliable asset.

Another journalist who secretly doubled as a CIA asset was *Newsweek*'s Arnaud de Borchgrave, who later became editor-in-chief of the conservative *Washington Times*. "He ran with anything we gave him and he shared everything he picked up along the way," Snepp said. Wendell S. "Bud" Merick, *US News & World Report*'s Saigon bureau chief from 1966 to 1975, was also "very friendly" to the CIA. "I don't think he was a paid asset, but he hung on every word," remembered Snepp. "Another incredibly important source of contact was Robert Shaplen of *The New Yorker*, who had fabulous sources." Then there was George McArthur, Saigon bureau chief for the *Los Angeles Times*, who dated and later married Eva Kim, the US ambassador's secretary. "George was her paramour and he had unparalleled access," Snepp recalled. "I served all these guys in various capacities but the main one was briefing the press. They had me in to tell them the deployment of forces, what have you. I was a kid, but I had the confidence of the ambassador and I was under a dictate to leak to the press what we thought would serve American interests."

During a cease-fire in 1974, a year before the war ended, Snepp began leaking intelligence that had been "cooked" to show South Vietnam was winning the war and was designed to persuade the US Congress to keep financing the lost cause. According to Snepp, it was easy to fool what little was left of the press in Vietnam because reporters had no way of verifying the CIA spin. "In the last days of the Vietnam War, we had the press in a box," he explained. "So journalists couldn't know the truth except as the CIA shaped it." With the North Vietnamese Army (NVA) barreling south, few reporters dared to go out in the field. "They were utterly dependent on us for embassy or CIA handouts," according to Snepp. "They were slaves to our information. And more to the point, we routinely tapped the [Saigon] bureaus' field lines to *US News & World Report* or wherever, so we knew what they were writing and then could tailor a briefing if we saw a soft spot in their perception of the situation."

After the war ended, the CIA tried to cover up how it continued its campaign of misinformation until literally the day Saigon fell to the North Vietnamese. "We tried to bury it all," he said. "We buried everything that happened. The CIA and Ford White House laid out a propaganda campaign that the communists had changed their plans at the end of the war. The CIA was lying to the press and lying to Congress. Kissinger was lying, and the Ford administration was misrepresenting what happened. It made me so angry. That's why I left the agency."

* * *

The Family Jewels file, which Colby had kept locked in his office safe, remained a secret until four months after his resignation the following year, on December 2, 1974, when Seymour Hersh broke the story in the *New York Times*. Under a banner headline, accompanied by grim-looking official photographs of Helms, Schlesinger, and Colby, Hersh revealed, "The Central Intelligence Agency, directly violating its charter, conducted a massive, illegal domestic intelligence operation during the Nixon Administration against the antiwar movement and other dissident groups in the United States, according to well-placed government sources."

The bad news for the CIA continued the following year, as Congress, led by Senator Frank Church of Idaho and Representative Otis Pike of New York, opened official probes into agency wrongdoing. The two congressional investigations produced eighteen separate reports of government lawbreaking. In the wake of the Church and Pike reports, Congress prohibited the CIA from planning or carrying out assassinations (a ban that would later be lifted by President Ronald Reagan), and placed the agency under congressional supervision, thus creating both the House Permanent Select Committee on Intelligence, which came out of the Pike Committee, and the Church Committee's successor, the Senate Select Committee on Intelligence. Among the reforms foisted on Langley: no longer could the CIA directly recruit American journalists, fund or otherwise infiltrate domestic news media, or carry out propaganda operations directed at the American public.

In August 1975, while making the Washington media rounds following his investigation, Church made it clear that the CIA was not the only Orwellian threat to US democracy. Though he didn't mention the NSA by name, he warned the American people about the obscure agency's alarming—and growing—technological powers. "In the need to develop a capacity to know what potential enemies are doing, the United States government has perfected a technological capability that enables us to monitor the messages that go through the air," Church said on NBC's *Meet the Press*, nearly four decades before Edward Snowden issued his own warning. "We must know, at the same time, that capability at any time could be turned around on the American people, and no American would have any privacy left, such is the capability to monitor everything—telephone conversations, telegrams, it doesn't matter. There would be no place to hide."

After more than a generation of unchecked power, America's intelligence empire had been severely humbled by the embarrassing revelations produced by investigative journalists and congressional watchdogs. Yet the US media's brief experiment with aggressive reporting on the national security state would prove to be short-lived. In the 1970s, hard-hitting reporters like Bernstein and Hersh were heralded by the public and pampered by their editors. Hollywood turned muckraking journalists into cultural icons. But by the early 1980s, with the triumph of the conservative backlash led by Ronald Reagan, journalists who questioned authority too much or seemed overly inquisitive were no longer in fashion in the media industry. As reporters would soon discover, speaking truth to power could ruin their careers.

* * *

One of the most extreme examples of CIA and White House media manipulation in the 1980s involves the Nicaraguan contras. The rebel army was formed in Honduras in the wake of Nicaragua's 1979 Sandinista revolution, and while described by Reagan as "freedom fighters," they were in reality nothing more than a CIA-trained and funded paramilitary force. The group's democratic face was Edgar Chamorro, a former priest and Harvard graduate from Nicaragua's prominent Chamorro family. After initially supporting the Sandinistas, Chamorro fled Nicaragua after the revolution and set up a public relations firm in Miami, which is where the CIA recruited him to become the official press spokesperson for the so-called Nicaraguan Democratic Force's (FDN) newly formed directorate. The CIA was hoping that the PR-savvy Chamorro could help clean up the image of the contras, who quickly developed a richly deserved reputation for thuggery and drug-running.

As Chamorro recounts in his 1987 book *Packaging the Contras*, the CIA saw him as a "useful tool," with an agency handler carefully rehearsing him in advance of press conferences, and stressing above all else that he should always deny the contras were receiving US funding. "One advisor said to me, 'Let's say a reporter asks you, Mr. Chamorro, do you receive money from the US government,' what will you say?'" he explained. "My initial response was to say, 'Yes, we have received some money. . . .' But I was told to say no, to say that we had received money from many concerned individuals, from people who supported our work but who would remain anonymous because they had a right to their privacy."

The CIA also instructed Chamorro to deny that he or other contra leaders had met with US officials, or that the contras had any intention of overthrowing the Sandinista-led Nicaraguan government. Instead, the contra front man was told that he should inform the press that the rebel group simply hoped to "create the conditions for democracy" in Nicaragua. Chamorro's first press conference took place at the Hilton Convention Center in Fort Lauderdale, Florida, on December 7, 1982. As the CIA had predicted, the assembled journalists hammered him with questions about covert US support for the contras. The reporters "asked precisely the questions that we had been told they would ask," he stated. "I, as the spokesperson for the Directorate, answered just as directly with responses that were often, in fact, quite untrue."

The CIA's disinformation strategy quickly paid dividends. "Directorate members denied the reports of CIA backing for FDN commandos and declined comment on military activities, saying they did not wish to violate US neutrality laws," the *Miami Herald* reported on December 8, the day after the press conference. The next day, the *New York Times* followed up with an exclusive interview with Enrique Bermudez, another contra leader who told the *Times* that "he was reluctant to talk while in the United States about military operations because American law, specifically the Neutrality Act, prohibits privately organized efforts to overthrow foreign governments." Again, the charade was maintained that the contras were drawing funding from many private sources, instead of being clients of the Reagan administration.

After helping the CIA launch the contra public relations campaign, Chamorro signed a six-month, $300,000 contract with the agency through a front company and opened an office in Tegucigalpa, Honduras. He prepared a "fact sheet" summarizing talking points for media interviews, flush with buzzwords, to describe the threat posed by the Sandinistas, such as "regional Soviet interests," "foreign agents," and "totalitarian." When Pope John Paul II visited Nicaragua on a tour of Central America in March 1983, arriving in country from the military-controlled Guatemala, he was heckled by a crowd denouncing President Reagan and shouting "Popular power!" and "We want peace."

The Pope responded with shouts of "Silence!" and scolded the Sandinistas for distancing Nicaraguans from their rightful bishops. The event did tremendous damage to the Sandinistas' image in the Catholic world, an outcome that the CIA may have had a hand in orchestrating.

Mirroring its strategy in Guatemala in 1954, when the CIA had overthrown the democratically elected government of Guatemala, the agency created a network of clandestine radio stations broadcasting into Nicaragua, as well as underground publications like *Comando*, a newsletter published by Chamorro, which featured images of contras posing with rifles in one hand and Bibles or crucifixes in the other.

Working with the CIA, Chamorro also assembled slick brochures promoting the contras in four languages, distributing them throughout Europe in a series of meetings with Christian Democrat politicians. As Chamorro explained, the meetings themselves were unimportant, and the intended targets of the propaganda weren't the Europeans, but the Americans: by showing that the contras were being welcomed by US allies, the meetings gave the appearance that the group had international legitimacy. "Another important element in the strategy of staging events whose repercussions would be felt in the US was the use of the European press," Chamorro adds. "We tried to get stories published in the European papers because we knew they would be reprinted or reported on in the US press."

From his base of operations at the Maya Hotel in Tegucigalpa, Chamorro met frequently with American and European news reporters covering the Nicaraguan civil war, giving special assistance to prominent US television networks, newspapers, and magazines like *Time* and *Newsweek*. While *Time* was reliably pro-contra, *Newsweek*'s coverage was more critical, but Chamorro points out that by simply paying attention to the contras, *Newsweek* helped make them more newsworthy than they otherwise would be.

On June 20, 1983, Chamorro met with *Los Angeles Times* reporter Dial Torgerson and freelance photographer Richard Cross, assisting them with directions on how to reach front lines. The next day, the two men died when a mine exploded beneath their car. Although the location of the blast on the Honduran side of the border, as well as the type of mine involved, pointed to the contras, press reports based on CIA disinformation blamed the Sandinistas. Both the *Miami*

Herald and the *New York Times* erroneously claimed the explosion had been caused by a rocket-propelled grenade fired from the Nicaraguan side of the border.

Chamorro eventually left the contras in 1984 after growing disenchanted with their political leadership as well as the military wing of the movement's miserable human rights record. For him, the last straw was a ninety-page CIA manual titled *Psychological Operations in Guerrilla Warfare*, which advised the contras on how to use "selective violence for propagandistic effects" and how to "neutralize" Sandinista officials. Ironically, the CIA had apparently created the pamphlet in an attempt to make the contras less indiscriminate in their use of terror, which the agency felt was counterproductive. Specifically, Chamorro claims, he quit after being overruled by other members of the FDN directorate when he tried to delete any mention of assassination in the CIA memo.

Chamorro also lamented what should have been his greatest moment as a propagandist: creating a real-life hero along the lines of Che Guevara whom the agency could hold up as a model contra soldier, thus attracting more US financial aid. After asking Bermudez for the names of the FDN's bravest fighters, he chose Pedro Ortiz Centeno, whose *nom de guerre* was "Suicida," or Suicide. Chamorro described Centeno, a former soldier in dictator Anastasio Somoza's brutal National Guard, as a "fanatically devoted warrior, almost crazy in battle." Both *Newsweek*'s James Lemoyne (who previously covered Vietnam for the *New York Times*) and the *Washington Post*'s Christopher Dickey were eager to run with the story. "The reporters thought they were using us to get a scoop; but we were using them to our advantage," Chamorro said. "Unfortunately for my plan, Suicida's brutality overshadowed his fighting ability, and his human rights violations became an embarrassment. In order to create the appearance of a concern for such violations of international law, Suicida was 'court-martialed.' By the end of the year, the man I thought was going to be the hero of the contras had been executed."

* * *

After the CIA's mishandling of the contras, the propaganda mission officially shifted from the agency to the National Security Council's Office of Public Diplomacy (OPD). But in reality the CIA was still running the show. Nominally headed by right-wing Cuban exile Otto Reich, the real brains behind the OPD belonged to Walter Raymond, one of the CIA's top propaganda experts, who was transferred from the agency to the National Security Council (NSC) in 1982. "They not only had this CIA guy running the whole show," observed Peter Kornbluh, a senior analyst with the National Security Archive, an independent research group at George Washington University, "they transferred US military psychological operations specialists to work in the office." OPD specialists scanned classified US embassy cable traffic for tidbits of intelligence on the Sandinistas or the left-wing rebels in El Salvador, and mined them for propaganda value. "They would write memos that would help press releases for articles that would float into the public domain and create negative publicity for the Sandinistas," Kornbluh explained.

The OPD represented a revolution in psychological warfare, not simply broadly disseminating propaganda to the general public, but specifically targeting reporters and editors. Previously, when the CIA handled such relationships, selling a story to a reporter was as simple as a phone call or a lunch date. But by the Reagan era, after the embarrassing exposés of press complicity, the CIA had to sell its propaganda to the press in different ways. Now getting favorable press involved sweet-talking, lobbying, or strong-arming journalists. According to Kornbluh, agency propaganda experts "explicitly put pressure on news outlets and specific reporters that were not reporting what they wanted."

During the 1980s, in military dictatorships like El Salvador and Guatemala, local journalists were routinely targeted for torture, disappearance, or execution. American reporters covering Central America were usually safe, but the work was inherently risky and stressful, and some reporters were driven out of the region with murder threats. In addition, reporters who wrote stories critical of the CIA or US policy in the region could expect to be "controversialized" by officials in the Reagan communications apparatus.

On one occasion, Kornbluh said that a pair of National Public Radio (NPR) reporters were viewed as too aggressive in their coverage of the Reagan wars in Central America. As a result, the reporters' stories were flagged, and Otto Reich paid a visit to the radio network's Washington headquarters to express the administration's strong displeasure.

The Reagan administration also brought strong pressure to bear on *New York Times* war correspondent Raymond Bonner and the *Washington Post*'s Alma Guillermoprieto after they exposed an elite, US-trained Salvadoran military battalion's brutal massacre of nine hundred unarmed villagers in the remote village of El Mozote. In response to the reporting, the White House went into overdrive behind the scenes, trying to convince as many influential reporters as possible that the stories were bogus, or that the Farabundo Martí National Liberation Front (FMLN) rebels had staged the massacre. The *Times* ultimately yanked Bonner out of the country and reassigned him to a business beat—although the newspaper never acknowledged a single error in Bonner's reporting, and both he and the *Times* insisted that his transfer was just part of the newspaper's typical policy of rotating most reporters from one beat to the next.

No US journalist earned the OPD's wrath as much as Associated Press reporter Robert Parry. In a recent interview, Parry recalled the first time he heard the word "controversialize." It came up, Parry said, in the mid-1980s in the middle of a friendly conversation with the OPD's Robert Kagan, now a prominent neoconservative intellectual and columnist for the *Washington Post*. "He was a young guy and very smooth," recalled Parry. "Even if he was sort of threatening you, he was funny about it." Because Parry was working for the AP's special assignment team, he frequently met with Kagan, who pitched him administration-friendly national security stories. "I would go check it out and if it turned out that it was exaggerated or wasn't really true, that wasn't what they wanted to hear. So I just refused to play and at one point, Kagan said, 'If you keep this up, we're going to have to controversialize you.' It was done in a light way, but it was how they thought. It was kind of a sophisticated press management operation."

Although Langley was no longer officially in charge of propaganda, CIA Director Bill Casey remained in the loop, kept up to speed by the OPD's Walter Raymond. The larger mission of Reagan administration propagandists was to convince the American public to overcome its post-Vietnam weariness and skepticism about overseas military intervention. "They actually would fret about this in their memos," Parry said. "They talked about America's 'hot buttons,' how to push them, and how they could divide us up into various segments to see how they could get us angry and worked up and ready to fight again. So there might be a theme they'd use for Catholics, a theme they'd use for lawyers, a theme for people in the Southwest, a theme for Jews." Parry recalled one particular OPD press release claiming to provide evidence that the Sandinistas were anti-Semitic. "It was very effective, but it turned out it wasn't true," he said. "I got hold of a classified cable from the embassy saying, 'You can't say that; it's not true.' But they classified the cable and went ahead with it anyway. That's the kind of thing they would do."

Another favored OPD technique originated with the CIA in the 1950s: spreading stories that demeaned foreign leaders who were seen as too defiant of Western power. Parry learned about this when he interviewed Miles Copeland Jr., the legendary CIA spy (and father of Stewart, drummer for the rock band The Police). "He was living in this little town outside of Oxford, [England]," Parry recalled. "He was very gregarious and his life was almost over." Copeland told Parry how the CIA, in 1953, had planted stories in the international press claiming that the target of their impending coup in Iran, President Mohammad Mossadegh, was an oddball, given to wandering around Tehran in a bathrobe. "He wore a robe, like they did [in Iran], but the CIA called it a bathrobe to make him seem eccentric and weird," Parry said.

The OPD's version of this tactic gradually became obvious when President Reagan repeatedly referred to Sandinista leader Daniel Ortega as the "dictator in designer glasses," because of Ortega's large-framed eyeglasses. "I never even understood that, frankly, because it's hard to find eyeglasses that aren't designer glasses," Parry pointed out. "But they'd create these caricatures of these different individuals for the press to pick up, and that's what Reagan called him."

According to Parry, the OPD knew that leaking convincing-sounding stories to reporters was far preferable to issuing official press releases. "They were sophisticated enough to know that if they made it sound like they were the 'deep throat' leaking it to you and it sounded like you were getting some really sensitive stuff, then not only was that good for you and you could impress your editor, but when it got out, the public would tend to believe it because it was coming supposedly from some guy who was leaking something and not from the government handing it out," Parry explained. "But it was the government handing it out."

By 1986, along with his reporting partner, Brian Barger, Parry had broken a string of major stories about the secret war in Central America, including a June 1985 AP article that was the first story to mention Oliver North's covert and illegal funding of the contras. Instead of cheering on Parry and Barger, however, their editors tried hard to diminish North's role in the story. Part of the reason, Parry knew, was the fact that North had been tasked with trying to free Terry Anderson, an AP editor in Beirut who had been kidnapped by Hezbollah in 1985. (Unlike William Buckley, the CIA Beirut station chief who was kidnapped in 1984 and died in captivity a year later, Anderson was ultimately freed in 1991.) "You had this strange set of relationships," Parry said. "Chuck Lewis, who was our bureau chief, was literally meeting with North and then coming back to review stories."

* * *

While reporters like Bonner, Guillermoprieto, Parry, and Barger were doing their best to uncover the truth about the Reagan administration's covert wars in Central America, often by reporting in perilous combat zones, the *Washington Post*'s Bob Woodward was stalking around Washington, D.C., gleaning classified information over lunches and dinners with CIA and White House officials. Woodward's 1987 book *Veil* arguably should have credited CIA Director Casey as a co-writer. Woodward knew Casey, a former OSS officer who had managed Reagan's first presidential campaign, well before Reagan appointed Casey to Langley's top job. For *Veil*, Woodward interviewed Casey "more than four dozen" times between 1983 and 1987. "We talked at his house, at his office, on plane rides, in corners at parties, or on the phone," Woodward wrote. "At times he spoke freely and explained his views. At other times he declined. . . . He once said, 'Everyone always says more than they're supposed to.'"

Woodward catalogued at least a half dozen cases where he and his editors at the *Post*, especially Ben Bradlee, held emergency meetings to determine whether to publish his latest national security scoop. For example, when the CIA became concerned that the Soviet Union had contingency plans to invade Poland, the agency leaked the information to Woodward in the hope that a *Post* article would preempt any such plan. However real or imagined the Soviet threat may have been, Woodward delivered the goods with an article titled "Concern Grows on Soviet Plans in Poland."

Then there are the stories the *Post* chose not to publish. In March 1982, Woodward—who had become a powerhouse at the newspaper in the years after he and Carl Bernstein had worked the Watergate beat—discovered that the CIA was covertly training and arming the contras. In Bradlee's view, the story was only news if the agency was doing so behind Reagan's back. "He said he wanted to go slowly, reminding me gently that the political climate was very different from the 1970s," Woodward recalled in *Veil*. "This is Reagan's government now, [Bradlee] said, and the presumption is no longer that the airing of CIA secrets is automatically good. It could be bad."

This is as succinct a statement of media subordination to Washington power as you will ever find. And the fact that it was Bradlee and Woodward—two 1970s icons of enterprising journalism—who were caving to this new mood of official intimidation, made it all the more disheartening. Though he always vehemently denied he had been a CIA asset, Bradlee had a long chummy relationship with the agency that dated back to his days as a press attaché in the US embassy in Paris in the early 1950s, and continued through many evenings on the Georgetown party circuit. And Woodward has long been rumored to have played an intelligence role during his service in the Navy in the 1960s, though he too denies this.

* * *

While Woodward and Bradlee fretted over what to do with the classified information that kept spilling from the lips of the likes of Casey, the AP's Parry and Barger were being pounded by rival newspapers and even their own editors. Whenever the AP published one of their stories, the arch-conservative *Washington Times* would print blind quotes from intelligence officials bashing their reporting. "They attacked us all the time," Parry said, adding that because Arnaud de Borchgrave, the CIA-friendly *Washington Times* editor, sat on the AP's board of directors, he couldn't just be blown off. "So I remember one of our editors had to go over to the *Washington Times* just to mollify them, so they wouldn't trash us anymore. They actually said, 'Please don't trash the AP on your front page anymore. We'll handle it internally.' That added to the pressure on Barger and me."

In summer 1986, after being reassigned to the overnight desk, the Siberia of the newsroom, Brian Barger finally quit the AP in frustration. "At that point, we'd been so beaten up on our stories, there was also a sense of why are we even doing this anymore," Parry recalled.

But then, in October 1986, the Sandinistas shot down a CIA cargo plane that had been illegally hauling weapons to the contras, parading the lone survivor, a hapless cargo handler named Eugene Hasenfus, before news cameras in Managua. At the same time, news broke of North's covert arms-for-hostages deal with Iran. "We had kind of been vindicated to some degree," Parry said. "But they wouldn't rehire Barger. They didn't recognize that this was the major story of the decade. They were living in their world, so they didn't get that they could change history, nor did they care."

When *Newsweek* offered Parry a job in 1987, he gladly accepted. But he soon regretted the move. Like the *Washington Post*, which owned the magazine, *Newsweek* had its own long history of cozy relations with the US national security elite, dating back to the Dulles days. "I didn't know how corrupt the organization was," Parry said. "What I was facing, which I didn't understand fully, was that Maynard Parker, who was the executive editor, really saw himself as part of the foreign policy establishment." Parker sat on the Council of Foreign Relations, an influential conclave of the power elite, and was friends with Henry Kissinger, who wrote a column for *Newsweek*. "Kissinger was close to [*Washington Post* publisher] Katharine Graham, who owned the publication," Parry explained. "Basically these editors were very much on the side of the Reagan people. And they had done a terrible job on Iran-contra up to that point. They had been dumping on it, not covering anything."

Although *Newsweek* had specifically hired Parry to beef up its coverage, his editors kept him on a tight leash. "When North's trial came around, they barred me from covering it," he said. So instead of attending the hearings, he reviewed the trial transcripts each night, gleaning details from bench conferences that other reporters weren't able to hear. Still, his editors refused to print his work, so Parry sneaked tidbits into the same *Periscope* section of the magazine that, ironically, the CIA had used for years to dump its disinformation and propaganda.

Despite the resistance from his editors, Parry still managed to expose one of the most important secrets of the Iran-contra era, a story that would eventually lead not only to the biggest journalism scandal of the 1990s, but also one of the worst public relations disasters the CIA had faced since the days of the Family Jewels fiasco. In 1985, after Federico Vaughn, allegedly a friend of a Sandinista official, was indicted in Miami for smuggling cocaine into the United States as a result of an elaborate sting staged by the DEA, President Reagan had publicly accused the Nicaraguan government of "exporting drugs to poison our youth." However, no convincing evidence ever emerged that the top leadership of the Sandinistas knew about Vaughn's smuggling or were otherwise involved in drug trafficking. In fact, as Parry and his AP reporting partner Barger discovered, it was the contras, not the Sandinistas, who were deeply involved in cocaine trafficking.

In December 1985, Parry and Barger penned the first story exposing what would later be called the "contra-cocaine connection." Their article described how planes flying cocaine from Colombia were landing at clandestine airstrips in contra-controlled territory in Costa Rica, where the planes would refuel and "transport cocaine to other Costa Rican points for shipment to the United States." Parry and Barger were able to confirm these reports when they obtained a top-secret National Intelligence Estimate prepared by the CIA alleging that one of the contras' top leaders "used cocaine profits this year to buy a $250,000 arms shipment and a helicopter."

Parry estimated that he had at least two-dozen separate sources for his contra-drug reporting. "You are dealing with a cast of characters that have problems," he said. "Nobody comes in as a perfect source on any of these things. They all have things to hide, to exaggerate; they have their agendas." Parry saw his job as exposing the elusive, underlying truth by weaving together as many perspectives as possible. "The idea was if you could get as many sources as possible, that would protect you," he explained. But the more sources Parry brought to the table, the more fodder he seemed to be providing for the OPD and its allies in the press to find one bad apple to discredit the entire bunch. "I used to joke that if you have two dozen sources, and one of them had a parking ticket when he was eighteen, then they'd throw the other twenty-three out."

Thus, rather than try to advance the story, the AP's competitors, including the *New York Times*, *Washington Post*, *Miami Herald*, and *Los Angeles Times*, printed follow-up articles that quoted anonymous government officials who were only too happy to discredit the allegations. "That was routine," Parry recalled. "First of all, having been beaten on a story? No one likes to admit that. Secondly, you can then go to your editors and say, 'My sources say this is a lot of crap,' so they either ignore it or put it down, and they did both in the case of the contra drug story. So instead of your story being confirmed by everybody, it is being ignored by everybody or it's being attacked, and now your editor is getting nervous."

In 1988, Parry teamed up with Peter Kornbluh from the National Security Archive and penned a story for *Foreign Policy* magazine that finally exposed the machinations of the Office of Public Diplomacy. Because it called out the blatant media manipulation game for what it was, the article won Parry no favors at *Newsweek*. After being yelled at one too many times by his editors, he finally quit the magazine in 1990.

Chapter Three

Killing the Messenger

S ix years after he quit *Newsweek*, Bob Parry received a telephone call from a journalist in California named Gary Webb. A veteran investigative reporter for the *San Jose Mercury News*, Webb told Parry that he had just learned the answer to the last major question of the contra-cocaine story: What had happened to all the drugs the contras were smuggling into the United States once they arrived north of the Mexican border? As Webb had uncovered in court documents, a group of Nicaraguan cocaine traffickers based in San Francisco had for years provided Los Angeles's most infamous crack peddler, "Freeway" Ricky Ross, with his most reliable supply of cheap cocaine.

Following on the heels of Parry's reporting about the contra-cocaine connection, Webb exposed a drug ring that included Ross's immediate supplier, Oscar Danilo Blandón Reyes—a Nicaraguan businessman whose family was well connected to the deposed Somoza regime—and the man who introduced Blandón to the drug trade, Norwin Meneses, a dapper, mustachioed trafficker known in Nicaragua since the mid-1970s as the "King of Cocaine." The US Drug Enforcement Administration (DEA) had been after Meneses since at least 1978, and had come close to taking him down in 1983 when agents busted a smuggling ring led by his associate, Julio Zavala. On January 17 of that year, several Nicaraguans wearing wet suits were arrested at San Francisco's Pier 96 as they attempted to unload more than four hundred pounds of cocaine from a Colombian freighter. Worth roughly $100 million, the seizure, now known to history as the "Frogman Case," was the largest made in California in the early 1980s.

Although Meneses was never charged in the case, drug agents knew he had ties to one of the Bay Area houses that were being used in the ring, and that he was the middleman who had brokered the deal for the Colombians. At Zavala's apartment, authorities seized $36,800 in cash and placed the drug money in an evidence bag for his trial. Then a strange thing happened: Zavala's Costa Rica–based attorney petitioned prosecutors to return the money because, he argued, it wasn't drug money after all, but rather funds that were given to his client to buy weapons and supplies to help achieve "the reinstatement of democracy in Nicaragua." In a pre-trial hearing, prosecutors held a closed-door meeting with the judge and, citing the Classified Information Procedures Act, sealed the letters in the case file, and then promptly agreed to release the cash to Zavala's lawyer. (The CIA later admitted that it had secretly intervened to have the cash returned to the contra fundraising pipeline.)

Following the Frogman Case, kingpin Norwin Meneses continued to operate in plain sight, seemingly untouchable. While working on the story for the *Mercury News*, Webb even managed to get ahold of a photo of a smiling Meneses standing next to Adolfo Calero, a Nicaraguan rebel leader handpicked by the CIA, at a 1984 contra fundraising dinner in San Francisco. By the time Webb began digging into the story a decade later, Meneses was serving a prison sentence for trafficking cocaine in Nicaragua, and Blandón, who Meneses had sent to Los Angeles to sell coke to African American gangs in the early 1980s, had become the DEA's go-to informant for criminal cases up and down the West Coast.

When Blandón showed up on the government's witness list at the trial of Freeway Ricky Ross, whom the *Los Angeles Times* had labeled the "kingpin" of crack cocaine, Webb couldn't believe his eyes. After all, by Blandón's own admission, it was he who had been Ross's biggest supplier in the 1980s. But the drug racket that Blandón set up with Ross, which helped spark Los Angeles's crack epidemic, also had a political dimension. In 1982, Blandón met in Honduras with contra military commander Enrique Bermudez, who instructed him to raise cash for the war against Nicaragua's Sandinista government by any means necessary. Blandón had no trouble understanding Bermudez's message. As Blandón later put it in a sworn statement, "The ends justify the means."

As Webb dug deeper into the Blandón-Ross drug ring, helped along by detailed accounts of its activities in court records, he found more evidence of its unusual rise to prominence in Los Angeles during the mid-1980s. Ross had been so successful in selling crack that authorities had to form a multi-agency task force specifically to take him down. But every time they raided a suspected stash house, they'd inevitably arrive a day too late—no drugs, no cash, just an empty room. Ross was always one step ahead of narcotics investigators, which meant that somebody had to be tipping off the drug lord and his henchmen. In October 1986, when officials conducted a major raid against Blandón and Ross, nearly every location they targeted had been mysteriously cleaned out ahead of time, leaving them with only small quantities of cocaine to seize as evidence.

One of the locations raided in the 1986 operation belonged to a former Laguna Beach police detective named Ronald J. Lister, who answered the door in his bathrobe, calmly sipping a cup of coffee. Lister indicated that he had been expecting the police to show up and that they were making a big mistake. "You're not supposed to be here," he explained, adding that he "worked with the CIA . . . and his friends in Washington weren't going to like what was going on." Inside Lister's closet, police found receipts and documents relating to his recent work as a globe-trotting arms dealer and security advisor to CIA-tied politicians in Latin America such as Roberto D'Aubuisson, the leader of El Salvador's death squads. As Blandón later told prosecutors, Lister—whom he had met at a contra fundraising event—not only had helped him launder the drug ring's money through a series of banks in Miami, but had also provided him with everything from machine guns to police radio scanners that he had, in turn, sold to Ross for use in protecting their drug network and evading capture.

As Webb described his findings over the telephone, Parry quickly recognized that the *San Jose Mercury News* reporter was on to an important aspect of the story he and Brian Barger had begun developing years earlier. "We had written about the external operation, and he was showing the consequences of what happened, how bringing cocaine into the US contributed to the crack problem," Parry said. "We had not looked into that." But Parry warned Webb about the story's radioactive history. "I asked him how his relationship was with his editors," Parry recalled. "He asked me what I meant. I said, 'You will be facing a serious counterattack, because this has happened to everyone who has ever written about it.' And he said he had a good relationship with his editors. He was naïve. He thought he had a good story, but he had no idea what he was about to set off or how his colleagues would go after him."

* * *

Parry's warning proved prophetic: just as he himself had been effectively "controversialized" in the 1980s, so soon was Webb, whose big story finally ran as a three-part *Mercury News* series in early August 1996. Titled "Dark Alliance," the series asserted that, by turning a blind eye to Nicaraguan drug smugglers who were helping the CIA raise money for the contras, the agency had played a direct role in the explosion of crack cocaine in South Central Los Angeles and elsewhere in the 1980s. Because it was the first blockbuster exposé published not just in print, but simultaneously on the Internet, Webb's story made a wide impact. By November 1996, millions of people had read the articles online, and outraged African American political leaders on Capitol Hill led by Maxine Waters, the Democratic US congresswoman from Los Angeles, were demanding an investigation. Although the nation's leading newspapers seemed intent on ignoring the explosive story, it became impossible for them to do so. Nightly news coverage of inner-city protests eventually culminated in an historic and ill-advised appearance at a South Central town hall meeting by CIA Director John Deutsch, who, through clenched teeth and to loud jeers from the crowd, promised to get to the bottom of Webb's allegations.

For a while, it appeared that Webb's reporting was forcing the mainstream media to do its job, as reporters were assigned to investigate various aspects of the Dark Alliance network. NBC News sent a team to Nicaragua, where they filmed interviews with Meneses and others for a *Dateline* segment. As Webb later told journalists Alexander Cockburn and Jeffrey St. Clair, who wrote about Webb in their book, *White Out: The CIA, Drugs and the Press*, one of the *Dateline* producers expressed shock that the agency's involvement with contra coke peddlers had been so effectively buried.

"Why hasn't this shit been on TV before?" the producer wondered aloud.

"You tell me," Webb answered. "You're the TV man."

However, as recounted by Cockburn and St. Clair, a few weeks later, *Dateline* backed off the story. And NBC News correspondent Andrea Mitchell—the domestic partner of Alan Greenspan, then Federal Reserve chairman, and a Beltway journalist deeply embedded in the Washington power world—began telling TV viewers that Webb's story was a "conspiracy theory" that had been "spread by talk radio." (Labeling unwelcome investigative reporting a conspiracy theory was, and remains, a favorite way of discrediting and dismissing aggressive journalism, dating back to the 1960s when the CIA advised its media assets to counter stories that questioned the official version of the Kennedy assassination in this way.)

Soon the mainstream media backlash against Webb was in full swing. Acting as if they were Langley's public relations departments, the *Washington Post*, *New York Times*, and *Los Angeles Times* published front-page rebuttals of Webb's work, exaggerating flaws in his reporting and calling out the way his editors had hyped the story, especially the eye-grabbing image of a crackhead inhaling smoke from a pipe that was superimposed over the official seal of the CIA. Based almost entirely on anonymous quotes from current and retired government officials, the newspaper stories denied that the Nicaraguan drug ring Webb had exposed played a prominent role in *contra* support circles or the US drug trade.

The most aggressive counterattacks came from the *Los Angeles Times*, which had been embarrassingly scooped by Webb, since his story had focused on the explosion of crack cocaine in Los Angeles, and thus had added motivation to go after "Dark Alliance." It did so with gusto: a three-day series of its own that actually contained more words than Webb's original articles. Perhaps the most egregious aspect of the paper's hit piece on Webb was the fact that it assigned Jesse Katz, the same writer who two years earlier had profiled Ross as the king of LA's crack empire, with the odious job of writing a new story taking away that crown. Now that Webb had revealed that Ross had been supplied by CIA-tied Nicaraguans, Katz conveniently argued that his original story on Ross was, in retrospect, somewhat overblown, and Ross was really just one of many major crack peddlers active at the time. The *Los Angeles Times*' revisionist follow-up profile of Ross was so obviously disingenuous that it only served to lay bare the depths to which the newspaper was willing to go in trying to protect its relationship with the CIA.

On the question of Ronald Lister and his alleged CIA ties, the *Times* eagerly quoted former associates of his who dismissed him as a "con artist" and portrayed his Latin American arms deals as the work of a bumbling imposter while simply taking the CIA's word that it had nothing to do with him.

In rushing to knock down Webb's reporting, the nearly two dozen reporters assembled by the *Times* to discredit "Dark Alliance" failed to do even the most basic investigative journalism required to get to the truth of the story. For example, as a reporter covering the story for both *OC* (Orange County) and *LA Weekly* at the time—the leading alternative newspapers in southern California—and without the vast resources of a major daily paper or television network, I still managed to uncover court and business records that clearly showed Lister's ties to a former CIA officer. And through Freedom of Information Act requests, I eventually obtained heavily redacted FBI and CIA reports demonstrating that Lister's extensive work in Central America during the Iran-contra era involved a former CIA operations chief. In addition, records revealed that the FBI, which investigated Lister's arms deals five times in the 1980s, had even questioned the CIA's former deputy director about his relationship with Lister. Although the details of that relationship remain classified, the reports made clear that while Lister was helping Blandón and Ross spread crack through southern California and beyond, he was also busy helping the CIA's covert wars in Central America.

Instead of acting like flacks for the national security state and burying Webb's work under an avalanche of official denials and self-serving assertions by anonymous CIA officials, the major newspapers could have advanced Webb's important, but incomplete, reporting by following his tantalizing leads and filling in his gaps. There was a defensive quality to the unrelenting press criticism of "Dark Alliance," as if reporters saw in the series an implied criticism of their own professional failure to expose the sins of the intelligence system. Many of the national security reporters and editors who were involved in the attacks on Webb had covered Reagan's Central America wars in the 1980s, including Doyle McManus, the *Los Angeles Times'* Washington bureau chief, and many of them were familiar with the allegations of contra drug smuggling raised in Webb's work. Thus, part of their critique of "Dark Alliance" stemmed from, as McManus later told me, a sense that "most of the elements of the story that had appeared new and significant on first reading were either not new, not significant, or not supported by real evidence."

Yet like most of the US mainstream press during the 1980s, McManus had allowed the CIA and White House officials to spin him into printing stories about Central America that were purely propaganda—only occasionally, when obvious facts on the ground contradicted official proclamations, publishing articles that challenged the assumptions of the national security state. In fact, the main reason Webb's reporting about CIA ties to crack sales proved to be so explosive is that the major newspapers that should have been covering that story during the 1980s had either ignored it altogether or buried it in their back pages, while the few reporters like Parry who dared to dig more deeply were swiftly taken off the story by their editors.

Spearheading the *Washington Post*'s assault on "Dark Alliance" was the paper's veteran national security reporter, Walter Pincus, who in the early 1950s had briefly worked as a CIA informant, spying on an international student summit in Vienna. Later, he tried to downplay this episode, comparing his stint as a spook to nothing more than a "college weekend with the Russians," and claiming that he didn't know it was the CIA that had recruited him. Nonetheless, Pincus—who retired from the *Post* at the end of 2015 at age eighty-three—was widely considered by press colleagues, including some in his own newsroom, as one of those Beltway warhorses who built his career by carrying water for the CIA, consistently filing stories that betrayed an intelligence insider's perspective, and loudly complaining to *Post* editors whenever the paper published a story he felt was harmful to national security interests.

Douglas Farah served as the *Washington Post's* correspondent in Nicaragua in 1996 when "Dark Alliance" broke. Farah recalled that his own reporting from Nicaragua bolstered Webb's work, but he couldn't get any traction with his editors, who already had their minds made up about the story. "One of my big fights on this was with Pincus," Farah said, "and my disadvantage was that I was in Managua and he was sitting in on the story meetings [in Washington] and talking directly to the editors. And we had a disagreement over the validity of what I was finding. At the time, I didn't realize he had been an agency employee for a while. That might have helped me understand what was going on there a bit."

At first, the *Mercury News* stood by "Dark Alliance," but in May 1997, executive editor Jerry Ceppos—facing his own possible career demise—gave in to the unrelenting criticism from the press fraternity and published a mea culpa backing away from the series. Webb resigned soon thereafter and never again worked in daily journalism. As I wrote in my 2006 book about Webb, *Kill the Messenger*, the scandal not only destroyed his career but ruined his life, leading him into economic hardship, depression, and a downward spiral of alienation from friends and family that ended with his suicide exactly seven years to the day after he had resigned from the *Mercury News*.

* * *

Even in death, the attacks on Webb continued. In its December 12, 2004, obituary of Webb, the *Los Angeles Times* dismissed him as the author of "discredited" work. But by then, it was Webb's press critics who were discredited. In January 1998, the CIA published its own Inspector General's (IG) report on "Dark Alliance," in which the agency acknowledged that for more than a decade, Langley had allowed the Nicaraguan contras and their fundraising partners to smuggle drugs into the United States. Furthermore, stated the IG report, the CIA had never shared this information with law enforcement authorities, and only punished contra drug traffickers on those rare occasion when the smugglers flagrantly disobeyed the agency's instructions. Ironically, the CIA's own internal report revealed far more agency complicity with drug dealers than "Dark Alliance" had ever suggested.

And yet, while the CIA might have been prepared to confess its sins, the press establishment was not. The agency's mea culpa went almost completely ignored by a national news media that was obsessed at the time with the sordid details of the just-breaking Bill Clinton–Monica Lewinsky sex scandal. Noticeably silent on the CIA's remarkable confession were the newspapers that had taken the lead in tearing down Gary Webb, namely the *Los Angeles Times, Washington Post,* and *New York Times.*

The CIA also conducted an internal study on the "Dark Alliance" controversy that revealed how the agency had worked with the mainstream press to ruin Webb's reputation. This report, which the agency titled "Managing a Nightmare," was originally prepared in 1997 but not released until October 2004—two months before Webb's death. In the report, the agency described how, in a rare departure from CIA policy of never commenting on covert operations or overseas assets, intelligence officials went public to deny its relationship with specific individuals mentioned in Webb's story. "Managing a Nightmare" also revealed that the CIA had undermined Webb by talking "one major news affiliate" out of covering the story. In addition, the agency's public

affairs office provided reporters as well as former CIA officials with "more balanced stories" that they could use as
talking points for attacking Webb. But for the most part, the
CIA report claimed, the agency simply sat back and watched
while Webb's own press rivals tore apart "Dark Alliance."

Without crediting Walter Pincus by name, the CIA gave
highest kudos to the *Washington Post* for the anti-Webb
backlash. "Because of the *Post*'s national reputation, its articles especially were picked up by other papers, helping to create what the Associated Press called a 'firestorm of reaction'
against" Webb and his story. For the CIA, seeing the nation's
leading news media not only assail Webb's work, but launch a
prolonged attack on the reporter himself, was nothing short
of miraculous. "This success has to be seen in relative terms,"
the agency concluded. "In the world of public relations, as in
war, avoiding a rout in the face of hostile multitudes can be
considered a success."

On August 14, 1998, a few months after the CIA released
its bombshell Inspector General's report that essentially
cleared his name, Webb went on C-SPAN to promote his
just-published book, *Dark Alliance*, which expanded on
his original series. Because the media had ignored the CIA
confession about the contra-cocaine connection, Webb's
career remained in a shambles. But it was clear from this
C-SPAN appearance that Webb's journalistic instincts were
still sharp. The show featured callers from around the country who seemed much more interested in President Clinton's
sex life than the CIA-drug scandal. But one of the last callers
focused on another intriguing national security story. The
caller asked Webb to comment on a front-page *Los Angeles
Times* story that had appeared that morning concerning an
exiled Saudi Arabian "dissident" named Osama bin Laden.
According to the *Times*, bin Laden, who was suspected of

responsibility for a pair of terrorist bombings on US embassies in Tanzania and Kenya, had turned against his homeland after it allowed US troops to use Saudi Arabia as a staging ground for Operation Desert Storm.

Webb told the C-SPAN caller that the *Times* story reminded him of the book *Endless Enemies* by *Wall Street Journal* reporter Jonathan Kwitny. "When we intervene in the affairs of other countries and we shoot at people, and people get shot with American guns and American bullets, we create enemies," Webb argued. "And if it is true that this man turned against the United States because of Desert Storm, we've created another enemy there that we might not have had before."

It was one more astute observation by Webb about the dark world of US national security affairs, and it was promptly lost in the media babble. For a fleeting moment, it underscored what a loss it was when his colleagues drove Gary Webb out of a profession that was sorely in need of journalists with the courage to peer through Washington's fog of disinformation.

Chapter Four

Embedded

If there was any hope that the Washington press corps would learn from its shameful servility during the Reagan era and become an aggressive watchdog over the national security state, that hope was crushed by President George W. Bush's Middle East follies—the ongoing nightmare that began with the March 2003 US invasion of Iraq. The Bush-Cheney administration's compulsion to jump off that cliff, taking much of the world with it, was vastly assisted by a codependent media. And it was not just the usual suspects, like Fox News and the *Wall Street Journal*, that cried out to unleash the hounds of war. Liberal beacons of the press like the *New York Times* also bear major responsibility for this epic fiasco.

As soon as President Bush announced his war on terror following 9/11, the floodgates of official misinformation opened and the US news media became a willing partner in the dissemination of a torrent of propaganda unseen since the early days of the Vietnam War. So powerful was the tide of disinformation flowing from the Bush-Cheney propaganda machine during the run-up to war that even the CIA caved under the pressure. Agency analysts knew that Saddam Hussein's WMD (weapons of mass destruction) assembly line no longer existed. But CIA officials soon fell in line with the White House's war fever, and helped give Bush his pretext for war.

Former intelligence officers and journalists who covered the buildup to the Iraq War concur that George Tenet, CIA director under both Bill Clinton and George W. Bush, lacked the leadership skills necessary to stand up to the steady stream of poorly sourced, unverifiable, or completely phony intelligence reports that were being cooked up and circulated within administration circles and leaked to the press. "I think the leadership at the CIA didn't stand up to the Bush administration and tell them what they thought," said James Risen of the *New York Times*. "They were so locked in to a certain belief system that they didn't process the information that said the opposite of what they believed. I think they assumed they'd find [the WMD] once they got there, and they were very mistaken. It was a very weird moment in history."

The definitive history of how the US media failed to do its job both before and during the war in Iraq can be found in *So Wrong for So Long*, a 2008 book consisting of more than seventy-five magazine articles about Iraq compiled by Greg Mitchell for *Editor & Publisher*. Beginning in early 2003, Mitchell became one of the few columnists to consistently question the claims being made about Iraq. As Mitchell's book shows, while warning voices about the looming war could be found in some magazines and online publications, the mainstream press overwhelmingly bought into the Bush administration's prewar propaganda.

In the newspaper industry, there was little questioning of the administration's war mania, with the notable exception of the Knight-Ridder chain. Some of the most bellicose and misleading reporting and editorials came out of the nation's two leading papers, the *New York Times* and *Washington Post*—newspapers whose complicity with the national security agenda dates back to the era of Cold War spymaster Allen Dulles. "There was an attitude among editors: Look, we're going to war, why do we even worry about the contrary stuff?" Thomas Ricks, a military reporter for the *Post*, told Mitchell.

In the days before the invasion, Ricks' colleagues, Karen DeYoung and Dana Priest, filed a story with their editors that raised doubts about Bush administration claims that Saddam was attempting to purchase uranium for a nuclear weapons program, but the *Post* sat on the story until after the war had begun. "We are inevitably the mouthpiece for whatever administration is in power," an understandably angry DeYoung told Mitchell.

After the shooting started, the *Washington Post's* editorial position remained hawkish throughout the war. Mitchell noted that the paper "not only continued to carry columns by several regulars who had repeatedly misfired on the war—and mocked antiwar critics—but it even went out and hired [as an editorial columnist] Michael Gerson, President Bush's main speechwriter during the run-up to the invasion." William Kristol, one of the neoconservatives most responsible for advocating Iraqi regime change, was a prolific columnist for the *Post*, often penning opinion pieces whose claims, Mitchell observed, ran "contrary to virtually everything emerging in the paper's own news pages." Only after the Iraq War became a quagmire did the *Post* begin to question its own coverage, with the paper's media critic Howard Kurtz acknowledging that while 140 front-page stories had focused on the case for war, opposing viewpoints simply "got lost."

* * *

Despite its best efforts, when it came to selling the war in Iraq, the *Washington Post* still came in second behind the *New York Times*. That's because the *Post* didn't have reporter Judith Miller. During the crucial six months leading up to the invasion of Iraq, the *Times* ran the most influential—and, as it turned out, completely indefensible—front-page stories that helped build the case for war. And almost all of them were written or co-written by Miller. In her 2015 memoir, *The Story*, Miller does her best to spread the blame for her discredited reporting, even citing the death of her father as a factor in her failure to follow the right clues. As she recalls in the book, Miller's odyssey from *Times* reporter to Bush war propagandist began when she bumped into the infamous Iraqi exile leader and fabulist Ahmed Chalabi—who would become the source of much of Miller's disgraced reporting—at an airport baggage carousel in November 2001. While waiting for her luggage, Miller asked Chalabi if he had any new information about Saddam and his alleged WMD program. Chalabi told her he didn't, but two months later, he put Miller in touch with a defector from the Baghdad regime named Adnan Ihsan Saeed al-Haideri, who claimed he had "refurbished facilities throughout Iraq to enable Saddam to store radiological and other unconventional weapons."

Miller flew to Bangkok to meet Haideri and on December 20, 2001, the *New York Times* published her story on the front page. Haideri, Miller reported, "personally visited at least twenty different sites that he believed to have been

associated with Iraq's chemical or biological weapons programs." These secret locations included "underground wells,
private villas, and under the Saddam Hussein Hospital in
Baghdad." It was the beginning of Miller's terror campaign,
a drumbeat of alarming stories about Saddam's alleged
doomsday weapons program that would help pave the way
to war. But like much of Miller's reporting, the Haideri story
turned out to be false. After the war began, as the *Times* was
forced to explain in a sheepish note to its readers, Haideri
escorted US inspectors to the arms locations he had pin-
pointed for Miller, but they "failed to find evidence of their
use for weapons programs." During the war, Miller managed
to get herself embedded with a WMD inspection team, so
she got a firsthand view of the fruitless search, much to the
growing chagrin of her editors.

No journalism, if that is what it can be called, played a
more significant role than Miller's in providing the Bush
administration with a rationale for war, as White House
spokespeople made the media rounds warning of a possible
"mushroom cloud" over our future unless the United States
took decisive action. By far the most important (and infamously wrong) of Miller's prewar WMD stories ran under
a banner headline on the front page of the *Times* and concerned Hussein's purported efforts to secure "thousands" of
aluminum tubes to make nuclear weapons.

"More than a decade after Saddam Hussein agreed to
give up weapons of mass destruction, Iraq has stepped up its
quest for nuclear weapons and has embarked on a worldwide
hunt for materials to make an atomic bomb," Miller and fellow *Times* reporter Michael Gordon reported on September
8, 2002, citing anonymous Bush administration officials.
"The attempted purchases are not the only signs of a renewed
Iraqi interest in acquiring nuclear arms. President Hussein

has met repeatedly in recent months with Iraq's top nuclear scientists and, according to American intelligence, praised their efforts as part of his campaign against the West."

Vice President Dick Cheney went on television the same day as her aluminum tube story appeared to cite her supposed findings as evidence of Saddam's treachery. "We do know, with absolute certainty," Cheney claimed, that Saddam is attempting "to build a nuclear weapon."

In an interview with CNN's Wolf Blitzer that led to headlines around the world, Condoleezza Rice, Bush's national security advisor, took the rhetoric all the way to the stratosphere, using lines written by Gerson, Bush's speechwriter and future *Washington Post* staffer. "The problem here is that there will always be some uncertainty about how quickly he can acquire nuclear weapons," Rice proclaimed. "But we don't want the smoking gun to be a mushroom cloud."

Miller's stories were finally rebuked by her own paper in May 2004—more than a year after the US invasion of Iraq—but the brief editors' note, which was buried deep inside the paper on page A10, was the mildest of mea culpas. None of Miller's editors, including executive editor Howell Raines and his replacement Bill Keller, were singled out for blame for what amounted to a colossal failure not only of reporting, but of editorial judgment. In its blandly worded "From the Editors" note to readers, the *Times*, in a stunningly self-serving understatement, conceded that Miller's reporting was "not as rigorous as it should have been," adding that unnamed editors who supervised the story "who should have been challenging reporters and pressing for more skepticism were perhaps too intent on rushing scoops into the paper."

Keller, who took over the newspaper's helm in July 2003, had been a major advocate for military action while working as a *Times* columnist in the months before the war. After he was forced to publicly disavow Miller's reporting, Keller sought to downplay the significance of the *Times* debacle. He subsequently told the *Washington Post* that the *Times* had only published the editor's note because the WMD controversy had become an inconvenient "distraction" for the newsroom. "This buzz about our coverage had become a kind of conventional wisdom, much of it overwrought and misinformed," he told the *Post*.

Judith Miller's journalism career would end in ruins, but responsibility for the *Times'* disastrous prewar coverage went much deeper at the newspaper than one reporter. It was not just Miller who had been played by the Bush-Cheney war machine, it was the *Times'* editorial hierarchy. In her memoir, Miller recalls arguing with Keller over his draft of the paper's WMD retraction, saying that he was unfairly putting all the blame on her. She wanted to know why the *Times* wasn't also critiquing a story by James Risen and David Johnston, whose front-page story on WMDs had reported there was a "broad agreement within intelligence agencies that Iraq has continued its efforts to develop chemical, biological, and probably nuclear weapons" and was "still trying to hide its weapons programs from United Nations inspectors." And what about the fact that the newspaper had hired Chalabi's niece to run its Kuwaiti bureau before the war began? "Or Chris Hedges' forever-exclusive scoops on Iraq's alleged camps for training al-Qaeda recruits to hijack airplanes? His articles had relied on *three* [original emphasis] defectors provided by Chalabi." When Miller resigned, she signed an agreement not to disclose her dispute with Keller—the same was supposed to go for him—so she rightly felt betrayed when her former editor described having to retract her discredited stories as "one of the low points" in his career.

* * *

Ironically, some of the most accurate reporting about Iraq came from leaks within the CIA, where there was widespread resentment against the Bush administration—and particularly Vice President Cheney's office—over its manipulation of intelligence to justify war. Jonathan Landay, then a national security reporter with Knight-Ridder newspapers, was one of the few journalists who managed to puncture the Bush administration's pro–Iraq War propaganda—and he did so with the CIA's help. As the stories about Iraq and WMDs began to surface elsewhere in the press, Landay's sources at Langley were telling him that these leaks were coming from Bush administration officials, particularly those close to Cheney. In an interview, Landay recalled learning how Cheney's staff had cherry-picked CIA intelligence that suited their purposes, passing along reports that seemed to bolster the notion Saddam had WMDs, while ignoring other intelligence that undercut the administration's case for war.

For instance, the CIA came to the conclusion that Saddam's regime had nothing to do with the 9/11 attacks on America. Despite this, Bush administration officials leaked a report— already disavowed by CIA analysts—that alleged a pre-9/11 meeting between al-Qaeda hijacker Mohammed Atta and an Iraqi intelligence agent in Prague. The false story was picked up by the Reuters news agency, and from there spread to the front pages of the *Times* and other papers. "They weren't happy with what was going on with Cheney," Landay said of his CIA sources.

Another reporter who helped expose Cheney and company's false claims about Iraq is Michael Isikoff, now chief investigative correspondent for Yahoo News, who was then a national security reporter for *Newsweek* and the first journalist to debunk the phony Mohammed Atta in Prague story. "The CIA got the report from Czech intelligence," Isikoff recently recalled over lunch in Washington, D.C. "It was pitched by advocates of the war early on, and Cheney was citing it on *Meet the Press*." Because he knew the meeting, if real, would help justify a US invasion of Iraq, Isikoff kept digging into the story, finally demolishing it in a May 5, 2002, *Newsweek* article that revealed Czech intelligence officials admitted they were wrong about the meeting and that US officials were now certain Atta wasn't even in Prague when it was supposed to have happened. According to Isikoff, his ability to write that story came from sources within the CIA who were trying to counteract Cheney.

"Certainly on the al-Qaeda ties, the CIA pushed back on that front," Isikoff said. "And that came through in a lot of stories." Nonetheless, added Isikoff, Langley still didn't have its hands clean on the Iraq War. In fact, what Isikoff calls the "single most fraudulent intelligence" on Saddam's so-called support of al-Qaeda came from statements made to the CIA by Ibn Shaykh al-Libi, a Libyan national. After being captured in Afghanistan in November 2001, al-Libi was tortured in Egypt where he told his interrogators that Saddam had been training al-Qaeda terrorists in the use of chemical weapons. After Tenet signed off on the report, Secretary of State Colin Powell incorporated the CIA's information about al-Libi into his February 5, 2003, speech to the United Nations Security Council, in which Powell infamously claimed to have evidence of an Iraqi WMD program. "It was completely a fraud," Isikoff said. "Al-Libi himself retracted it." In 2006, the CIA flew the inconvenient al-Libi to Libya, where three years later, he supposedly killed himself in one of Muammar Gaddafi's dungeons for political prisoners.

Powell's fraudulent UN speech in February 2003 proved to be the defining moment of the Bush administration's successful propaganda campaign to convince the US media and the general public to support military intervention in Iraq the following month. The American press rushed to embrace Powell's performance, though it would later be revealed as the biggest disgrace in the soldier-statesman's career. As Greg Mitchell would recount, "CNN's Bill Schneider said that 'no one' disputed Powell's findings. Bob Woodward, asked by Larry King on CNN what happens if we go to war and don't find any WMDs, answered: 'I think the chance of that happening is about zero. There's just too much there.'" Across the country, Mitchell added, newspapers called Powell's performance "powerful . . . a sober, factual case" (*New York Times*), "impressive in its breadth and elegance" (*San Francisco Chronicle*), "overwhelming" (*Tampa Tribune*), "devastating" (the *Oregonian*), "masterful" (*Hartford Courant*).

The *Washington Post* editorial went so far over the top in its support for Powell's war argument that it sounded like it had been written in Cheney's shop, declaring that "it is hard to imagine how anyone could doubt that Iraq possesses weapons of mass destruction," and that "only a fool—or possibly a Frenchman—could conclude otherwise."

There were those in the diplomatic community, however, who were not as credulous as the American press. Among these skeptics was Joseph Wilson, a former US ambassador and foreign service officer during the administrations of George H. W. Bush and Clinton. Powell's claim that Iraq had sought to obtain yellowcake uranium in the African country of Niger, material that could be used to manufacture a nuclear warhead, surprised the former ambassador. That's because in February 2002—a year before Powell's speech—the CIA had hired Wilson, who had extensive diplomatic experience in Africa, to go to Niger to investigate these claims. Wilson soon concluded there was no evidence to support the yellow-cake story, which he promptly reported back to the CIA and the State Department upon his return.

But Wilson was dismayed to see the discredited yellow-cake story continue to pop up as the Bush administration launched its drive for war, particularly in Powell's UN presentation, a man who enjoyed such wide respect and credibility. By the time that the administration unleashed its "shock and awe" assault on Iraq a month after the speech, Wilson was convinced that the American people had been duped. On July 6, 2003, he published a provocative op-ed piece in the *New York Times* titled "What I Did Not Find in Niger." "Based on my experience with the administration in the months leading up to the war, I have little choice but to conclude that some of the intelligence related to Iraq's nuclear weapons program was twisted to exaggerate the Iraqi threat," Wilson wrote.

It did not take long for the administration to strike back. A week after Wilson's article ran, Deputy Secretary of State Richard Armitage—passing along a leak that would later be traced to Lewis "Scooter" Libby, Cheney's chief of staff—told various Washington reporters that Wilson's wife, Valerie Plame, was a CIA employee. On July 14, 2003, conservative syndicated columnist Robert Novak published Plame's name in a *Washington Post* column titled "Mission to Niger," thereby blowing her cover, putting her network of assets at risk, and effectively ending her spy career. When Wilson went on television to denounce Novak and his administration cronies, the conservative press escalated its assault on the couple, despite their long, distinguished careers in service of Republican as well as Democratic presidents.

A criminal investigation ultimately led to the indictment and conviction of Scooter Libby, who avoided prison time thanks to a commutation of his sentence by President Bush. Ironically, the only person who did wind up behind bars was the *Times'* Judith Miller. Along with numerous other reporters, including the *Post's* Bob Woodward, Miller was ordered to name the officials who had given her Plame's name and CIA status. After refusing to name her sources, she spent eighty-five days in jail, an unfortunate episode that Miller milked in her memoir in an unconvincing effort to restore her credibility as a journalist.

According to the *Times'* James Risen, the government's prosecution of the Plame case made national security reporting, already difficult since 9/11, even more arduous. "Before 9/11 it was much easier to cover intelligence," Risen said. "The threat of leak investigations was much less, so there was none of the pressures people face today about criminal investigations and stuff like that. I think the Plame case made prosecutors feel they could make a name for themselves if they pursued these cases. Up until then, the government didn't want to go after reporters. They didn't go ballistic. It was a much more sane approach. The government realized we had a job to do and it was important for the people to know things even if they didn't like it. After the Plame case, things became much more of a war between the press and the government."

* * *

The truth, however, is that there were very few reporters on the national security beat like Risen who gave the Bush-Cheney administration any cause for concern. When the US invaded Iraq on March 20, 2003, much of the American press began to function as if they were the Pentagon's unpaid publicists. Just as the US military orchestrated press conformity during the Persian Gulf War, nearly all reporters covering the Iraq War found they had no choice but to "embed" themselves with US forces—military jargon for the Pentagon's post-Vietnam policy of only allowing reporters in combat areas if they were officially attached to a particular military unit. Not only were reporters, therefore, more limited in terms of their ability to serve as objective witnesses to the war, but they were also subject to both official censorship and the inevitable bias that comes with sharing a foxhole with your sources while being fired upon by the enemy.

"When you have the press in a hot box like we did in Vietnam and again in the Green Zone in Iraq, and whenever when the press is embedded, you are a hostage to the government," said former CIA officer Frank Snepp. "Like Judy Miller: she thought what she had was too good to be true and it was. When she started to get leaks about WMD, she was in the same box that reporters in Vietnam were in. They had no way to corroborate such rarified access, because they had no other intelligence. It's not that you own the press, it's that the press has no way of owning itself and is utterly dependent on handouts."

Although Vice President Cheney's office had spearheaded the propaganda effort that drove the United States into the Iraq fire pit, the Pentagon took over media manipulation once ground fighting began, just as it had done during the Persian Gulf War. This was done mostly by strictly limiting journalistic access to combat areas and thus preventing the public from seeing the type of horrifying imagery that had helped undermine US support for the Vietnam War.

Between September 1, 2004, and February 28, 2005, during which time nearly six hundred US soldiers died in combat, the nation's six largest newspapers ran "almost no pictures from Iraq of Americans killed in action," according to a survey by the *Los Angeles Times*.

Newspapers and television networks were even prevented from filming or taking photographs of flag-draped coffins being unloaded from the cargo holds of aircraft returning from Iraq. Meanwhile, as first exposed in 2005 by Jonathan Landay for Knight-Ridder, the US Army laundered payments through the Baghdad Press Club to pay Iraqi reporters to "produce upbeat newspaper, television, and radio reports" about the war. While not strictly illegal—the Pentagon can always justify propaganda operations when it can argue that doing so helps protect US boots on the ground—the officials involved in the program became worried that the ridiculous level of disinformation would backfire on the war effort, "undermining US credibility in Iraq" and potentially causing 'blow back' to the American public."

Yet the facts on the ground gradually began to speak for themselves, as the war in Iraq became a charnel house for US troops and Iraqis alike, with estimates of Iraqi civilian deaths numbering at least 123,000 in the first ten years of war—and hundreds of thousands more displaced, impoverished, and made sick from the environmental degradation of war. The war also set off a chain reaction that destabilized the region, leading to civil war and widespread suffering in Syria, and the rise of new terror groups like ISIS.

The Bush-Cheney administration's disastrous rush to war—with the shameful complicity of America's major media institutions—led to a deepening public distrust of official news sources. Fed up with managed news, people increasingly turned to maverick information channels like

WikiLeaks, the online clearinghouse for leaked national security information. Founded by Australian hacker Julian Assange, WikiLeaks first drew widespread attention when it posted horrifying footage recorded in July 2007 from the cockpit of a US Apache helicopter gunship flying above Baghdad. After the pilot reports over his microphone that he's watching a group of suspected insurgents who seem to be gathering near a vehicle, he casually shreds them to pieces with cannon fire. The "insurgents" turned out to be a group of Iraqi journalists who were simply trying to do their jobs. In 2010—stunned by footage like this and explaining "I just couldn't let these things stay inside my head"—a twenty-two-year-old US Army soldier named Bradley Manning provided WikiLeaks with more than three-quarters of a million classified documents, mostly military and diplomatic cables, which Assange began posting online for anyone to read.

Unsurprisingly, the national security state moved swiftly to punish both Manning and Assange. Manning, who now identifies as a woman (Chelsea), is currently serving a thirty-five-year prison sentence for leaking classified information, and federal prosecutors haven't ruled out filing similar charges against Assange. The WikiLeaks founder was forced to seek asylum in London's Ecuadorean embassy in 2012 when authorities tried to extradite him to Sweden on sexual assault charges—accusations that Assange insists were trumped up to deliver him into the hands of US authorities. In February 2016, a United Nations panel ruled in his favor, declaring that Assange was being "arbitrarily detained," and should be allowed to walk free from the embassy. But as of the publication of this book, Assange remains effectively under house arrest.

If whistle-blowers like Manning and Assange thought they could light a fire under the American press, that great slumbering watchdog, they were soon disappointed. Instead of rallying around them as heroes who had provided revealing insights into the secretive operations of America's perpetual war machine, the press treated them as dangerous and irresponsible interlopers on the media's turf. Newspaper editors like Bill Keller of the *New York Times* had no problem cherry-picking some of WikiLeaks's scoops, but they were quick to kill the messenger, running pieces that disparaged Manning and Assange. Keller even ridiculed Assange—a man forced to be constantly on the run from authorities, with no place to call home—for his lack of hygiene and grooming.

Some media outlets even coordinated their coverage of WikiLeaks with the Obama administration. When *60 Minutes* announced that it was going to interview Assange in early 2011, for example, Obama officials leaped into action, as evidenced by recently declassified emails from the office of then-Secretary of State Hillary Clinton. In a January 28, 2011, email, Philip J. Crowley, then assistant secretary of state for public affairs, told Clinton that he had a plan to undermine Assange's upcoming television appearance. "We had made a number of suggestions for outside experts and former diplomats to interview to 'balance' the piece," he told her. "*60 Minutes* assures me that they raised a number of questions and concerns we planted with them during the course of the interview. . . . We will be prepared to respond to the narrative Assange presents during the program."

Sure enough, *60 Minutes* interviewer Steve Kroft played hardball with Assange, at one point asking him if he was a "subversive" and "anti-American." He also accused Assange of "playing outside the rules" and thus couldn't expect to be protected by them. "And if they let you get away it, then they are encouraging . . ." Kroft continued, until Assange interrupted him.

"Then what? They will have to have freedom of the press?" Despite Kroft's attempt to question Assange's motives, he failed to throw his guest off his game. If the government succeeded in shutting down independent sources of information like WikiLeaks, Assange argued at the end of the interview, "The US has lost its way. It has abrogated its founding traditions. It has thrown the First Amendment in the bin. Because publishers must be free to publish."

As early as 2008, the US Army produced a report identifying WikiLeaks as an official enemy and detailing a strategy on how to target the people behind it. Classified National Security Agency documents leaked in 2013 by Edward Snowden, an NSA contractor, also reveal that the agency placed Assange on a "manhunting" list three years earlier, and had worked with British intelligence to monitor visitors to the WikiLeaks website.

* * *

Though only twenty-nine at the time, Ed Snowden proved to be a remarkably sophisticated young man when it came to analyzing power and the press. He was clearly well aware of how closely affiliated the corporate media is with the national security state. And so when Snowden, alarmed by the vast growth of the US surveillance system—which a dozen years into the war on terror, had turned every American into a suspect, as well as our allies overseas—decided to leak his treasure trove of classified documents, he sought out independent journalists Laura Poitras and Glenn Greenwald, instead of the *New York Times* or CNN. Although the London-based *Guardian* newspaper—where Greenwald's blog had shifted from *Salon*—as well as the *Washington Post* were brought in to ensure wide news impact (against Greenwald's wishes),

Snowden and his two independent news collaborators kept control of how and when to break the stories.

After collaborating on the explosive Snowden revelations, for which he won a Pulitzer Prize in 2014, Greenwald went on to launch his own online news site, the *Intercept*, with Poitras and investigative journalist Jeremy Scahill. Greenwald firmly believes that the media establishment is so deeply compromised by the national security state that building a robust independent press is the only way to ensure the free flow of information in America. In his book about the Snowden affair, *No Place to Hide*, Greenwald cites such examples of mainstream press subservience as the spiking of *New York Times* stories about illegal NSA surveillance as well as the *Washington Post's* 2005 decision to withhold the locations of the CIA's "black sites" from Dana Priest's blockbuster exposé, thus arguably allowing the agency to continue torturing detainees.

America's leading newspapers, Greenwald observes, are so close to the security agencies they cover that they end up adopting not just the government's perspectives and priorities but even its actual tone of communication. This, he adds, is why, outside of editorial pieces, newspapers like *Times* and *Post* shy from using the word "torture," for example. "The culture of US journalism mandates that reporters avoid any clear or declarative statements and incorporate government assertions into their reporting, treating them with respect no matter how frivolous they are," Greenwald argues. "They use what the *Post's* own media columnist, Erik Wemple, derides as *middle-of-the-road-ese*: never saying anything definitive but instead vesting with equal credence the government's defenses and the actual facts, all of which has the effect of diluting revelations to a muddled, incoherent, often inconsequential mess."

In a telephone interview that was interrupted several times by mysterious clicking and disconnections, Greenwald said from his home in Rio de Janeiro that he sees very little difference between the elite press and the government itself. "The established media in the United States is extremely close to the government and will react the same way the government does," he argued. "So if the government views a certain type of journalism as hostile, the media will too, because they are indistinguishable, as we saw with WikiLeaks and Snowden."

Greenwald cited his own treatment in the pages of the *Times* and *Post*, both of which published numerous opinion pieces questioning his motives as well as his status as a legitimate journalist. The original headline of the 2013 *Times'* profile story on Greenwald was "Anti-Surveillance Activist at the Center of New Leak." When he protested being dismissed as an "activist," the newspaper upgraded in its print edition to "Blogger, With Focus on Surveillance, Is at Center of a Debate."

"One would expect the government will attack journalists that shine light on illegal activities," Greenwald concluded, "but in the US, the government doesn't even have to do it because the media will do that for them."

The rise of whistle-blowers like Manning and Snowden, maverick sites like WikiLeaks, and independent journalists like Greenwald might have made life more difficult for national security overseers. But institutions like the CIA, Pentagon, and NSA still have enormous power to manage the news. In the next chapter, we will see how a journalist and a whistle-blower can team up to expose a shocking case of abuse at Guantanamo, win a major journalism award in the process, and still find themselves erased from the media picture.

Chapter Five

Cover-Up at Camp America

T he dust had barely settled at the lower Manhattan site of the collapsed World Trade Center towers in September 2001 when America's national security state began setting into motion a series of secret policies that would lead to seemingly endless war and the exponential growth of a global surveillance and detention system. The story of how the CIA, working in tandem with White House and Pentagon officials and handpicked constitutional lawyers, created a massive spying system, an "extraordinary rendition" (officially sanctioned kidnapping) program, and widespread "enhanced interrogation" (torture) at "black sites" (secret prisons)—all outside the framework of domestic and international law—has been well told. At the heart of this "extra-legal" system was the Guantanamo Bay Detention Camp, operated by the Pentagon on the oldest overseas US Navy base, at the southern tip of Cuba. Since this facility held some of the highest-profile prisoners and came under the most international scrutiny, Washington put a major effort into choreographing media coverage of "Gitmo."

"They used to bring us down there on these dog and pony shows to see how great the facilities were," said Brian Bender, *Politico*'s defense correspondent. Jason Leopold of *Vice News*, who has also made numerous trips to Guantanamo Bay, agreed that the experience was essentially a media circus. "I don't even know if you'd call it manipulation because it's just propaganda and brainwashing," Leopold said. "Guantanamo is a place where the military is simply trying to put out its version of how great Guantanamo is: 'Look at all these video games; look at all these books. Look at the meals! Taste the food we give to them.' Are you kidding me? These guys are in prison."

Predictably, many reporters who paid personal visits to the base have all too eagerly lapped up the military's propaganda that, if anything, the Guantanamo detainees are being treated too kindly. In his reporting on Guantanamo Bay, Leopold said he has been careful to avoid buying into the Pentagon's euphemistic press releases, which, for example, refer to leg irons as "humane restraints" and force-feeding, which is commonly used against hunger-striking detainees at the prison, as "enteral feeding." Leopold can't remember ever feeling so manipulated as a reporter than while at Guantanamo Bay. "Everything was staged; everything was rehearsed," he recalled. "They [rehearsed] what they were going to say; they told the guards what to say; they sat in on the interviews, wouldn't allow guards to answer questions. I have never seen more secrecy than I have when I visited Guantanamo Bay. It is a black hole."

On one trip, in 2013, when Leopold happened to be the only reporter touring the base, the Pentagon's metaphorical curtain briefly fell away from the stage when Leopold's military handler left him alone for a few minutes inside the Media Operations Center on the naval side of the base. "I'm in there by myself and see all these different cards spread on the floor," he recalled. Leopold picked up one of the cards and read both sides. *Holy shit*, he thought. "I scored. The trip is worth it just for this." What Leopold had in his hands was a "Public Affairs Smart Card" consisting of a set of instructions on what could and couldn't be shared with reporters.

Under the section "What You CAN Talk About" were catchphrases like "Mission: Safe, Humane Legal, Transparent," as well as suggested story pitches such as "[A] Day in the Life of a Guard." The card urged Gitmo spokespeople to "Own the Interview, Stay Confident," and "Stay in Your Lane," adding that under no circumstances was it permissible to discuss "high-value detainees," detainee "suicide," "attorney allegations," the "results of investigations," or "speculation on detainee release." Finally, the card urged prison media handlers to remember that "everything is on the record and to never say, 'No comment.'"

After Leslie Stahl and her *60 Minutes* camera crew won a tour of the prison that the CBS program billed as "unprecedented access," Leopold called the Pentagon's public affairs office demanding to know how this had been arranged. When the Pentagon refused to answer, Leopold filed a FOIA request demanding access to all emails and other correspondence relating to the *60 Minutes* visit. "When [other reporters] go to Guantanamo, we are not afforded great access," he complained. "You get to see a cell block. It's empty. We get to observe detainees at a distance." So Leopold couldn't believe his eyes when he saw the *60 Minutes* segment. *You've gotta be fucking kidding me*, he recalled thinking. "They showed Leslie Stahl walking down an active cell block with detainees yelling 'They are torturing us, get us out of here.' Access that was not afforded to us. How the fuck did this happen?"

Two months after making the FOIA request, Leopold received a call from the Pentagon public affairs office complaining that they were being forced to comply with his time-consuming request. "Can you explain to me why you're doing this?" the spokesperson asked Leopold. "Can you explain to me how you would feel if I was to say to you, 'I want to see all your emails?'"

Leopold responded by saying it was nothing personal. "I had no idea they were going to ask for all your emails. But I want to know how [CBS] got access."

According to Leopold, the Pentagon's public affairs office punished him by leaking information that he had requested to a rival reporter. "I had an FOIA for a document and the document that was eventually given to me was first given to my competitor at the *Miami Herald*," he said. "And the argument that was made was. 'Well, once we release it under FOIA, it's available to everyone.' Sure it is, I know that, but it's not usually the way it works. . . . That was payback."

* * *

Unlike most of Guantanamo Bay's prison guards, whose average age hovered somewhere around twenty years old, Joe Hickman was already in his thirties when he arrived on the island in 2006. A former correctional officer, Hickman enlisted in the army after 9/11, and upon completing airborne ranger training, he joined the Maryland National Guard, which is how he ended up at Guantanamo Bay. "It was a huge charade; it was absolutely ridiculous how we manipulated the press," Hickman recalled. Every time a reporter was scheduled to visit the prison, Hickman said the public affairs officers would begin preparing a week ahead of time. "Two or three days before the reporter arrived they would do rehearsals of where they were taking them," he said. "They would have guards playing the reporters. It was rehearsed to the tiniest detail."

In order to keep reporters from realizing how thoroughly scripted their prison tours were, the Gitmo public affairs officers would even practice supposedly spontaneous events, according to Hickman. "The public affairs officer would say, 'Why don't we head this way? Let's see what's happening here.' They did this the whole time." Hickman said that the only area of the prison complex where journalists were allowed to visit was the one reserved for compliant prisoners. "If some [prisoners there] were still mouthy, they would move them to maximum security cells prior to the reporters getting there. They filtered out the ones they were worried about. And if they did yell out, they'd be put in maximum security."

The one time Hickman can recall the Guantanamo public affairs staff getting nervous about a reporter's upcoming visit involved Ted Koppel, the well-respected former anchor for ABC's late-night news program, *Nightline*, who was working at the time on a three-hour special about the war on terror for the Discovery Channel, which later aired in September 2006. "Koppel scared the shit of them for some reason," Hickman said. "I don't know if they were afraid of information he had, but they practiced for two weeks every day." Conversely, only two days of rehearsals took place when Fox News's Bill O'Reilly showed up. "They knew from the beginning that O'Reilly would give them a good report."

As it turned out, the Pentagon had very little to fear from Koppel, who spent three days at Guantanamo only to depart with such penetrating observations as "the men all have long beards" and, just like prison inmates anywhere, "they don't look nearly so dangerous as they might if you were meeting them in a different situation in which they were holding a weapon." During an interview the TV news legend gave NPR about his documentary, when asked whether the prisoners seemed to be well treated, he responded blandly that they "look all right." The headline of a *New York Times* review of his show noted that, instead of asking the tough questions viewers might have expected, Koppel had essentially given "officials a cozy forum" to talk about terrorism.

Not only did the outside world have almost no real understanding of the conditions in Guantanamo Bay, but according to Hickman, the same was also true for most of the guards working inside the prison. For Hickman, all that changed one afternoon when he and another guard were conducting a mobile patrol along the perimeter of Camp America, a sprawling area that contains the much smaller Camp Delta, where the detainees are housed. While patrolling, Hickman spotted a secret complex nestled on a hillside. The facilities looked newly built, with aluminum siding. "I felt a really strange feeling in my gut," Hickman recalled. "It wasn't on any of our maps of the entire island. This place wasn't supposed to be there at all."

The guard who was with Hickman shared his suspicions. "You know what we just found?" he said. "We just found our Auschwitz." Hickman and the guard gave the secret facility the nickname "Camp No," as in "no such camp."

Not long after—on the evening of June 9, 2006—Hickman, while working his shift as Camp Delta's sergeant of the guard and standing duty in a thirty-five-foot tower, watched a prisoner being taken out of one of the detention blocks and placed in a white van that went in the direction of Camp No. The van returned twenty minutes later and picked up a second prisoner, and then a third. Shortly before midnight, the van returned and backed up to the medical clinic. That's when all the lights came on at the camp and the siren went off. Hickman approached a navy corpsman he knew from the medical clinic, who told him that three detainees had just died and that rags had been stuffed down their throats. The Pentagon issued a press release stating that, in an act of "asymmetrical warfare," the three detainees had committed suicide by simultaneously hanging themselves. But Hickman became convinced the men had been killed, perhaps accidentally, while being interrogated at Camp No.

* * *

After leaving the service, Hickman continued to investigate the mysterious Guantanamo deaths, with the help of researchers at New Jersey's Seton Hall University School of Law. Hickman and his research team found evidence that the dead prisoners had been subjected to unusually high doses of mefloquine, a powerful anti-malarial drug. Malaria doesn't exist in Cuba, and Hickman insisted that neither he nor any of the guards with whom he had served were inoculated against it. But he found evidence that mefloquine—which at high levels can cause psychotic reactions, including suicidal thoughts—was sometimes used on interrogation subjects by US security agencies.

In 2010, Hickman shared his story with journalist Scott Horton, who published a lengthy investigation of the detainees' deaths the following year in *Harper's* magazine, which won the 2011 National Magazine Award for reporting. Horton concluded that the three detainees did not commit suicide by hanging themselves with blankets, as the military claimed, but died—either accidentally or intentionally—while being tortured.

Despite winning the prestigious National Magazine Award, the Gitmo exposé met with stiff resistance from major newspapers and TV networks. Hickman, who by then had returned to civilian life with an honorable discharge, knew that with his spotless military record the Pentagon would have a difficult time discrediting him. "I had some of the highest ratings as an NCO [non-commissioned officer] you can get," he said. "When I was on duty in June 2006 [when the detainees died], for that quarter—April, May, and June—I was rated the best NCO in Guantanamo, and prior to going [to Cuba], I was soldier of the year for the whole year in the state of Maryland."

While this inoculated Hickman against any smear campaigns, it didn't prevent the press from ignoring his story. Veteran reporters like Brian Ross, head of ABC News' investigative unit, and Jim Miklaszewski, NBC News' chief Pentagon correspondent, interviewed Hickman and his Seton Hall Law School researchers, but suddenly dropped the story without explanation after talking to Pentagon officials.

Besides the *Harper's* award-winning cover story, the only exception to the media blackout of Joe Hickman's exposé was a December 2010 story by reporters Jason Leopold and Jeffrey Kaye in the online news site, *Truthout*. Leopold learned of Hickman while pursuing his own inquiry into the suspicious deaths of Gitmo inmates. By interviewing lawyers for detainees, Leopold had already learned of longstanding allegations of torture at the prison. So when he heard that three detainees had all supposedly committed suicide at the same time in an act of "asymmetrical warfare," he didn't believe it for an instant. "That was obviously a turning point in the history of Guantanamo Bay," Leopold said.

In 2008, Leopold discovered that a man named Scott Gerwehr—who said he worked for the CIA at the prison and had apparently just begun reaching out to reporters about what he knew—died in a motorcycle crash in Los Angeles. "I had learned he was working for the CIA, setting up the cameras there, doing what was called 'deception detection' during interrogations," Leopold recalled. "In the course of that investigation I learned that one person who may have information about him was Joe Hickman. So I reached out to Joe." During the course of their conversation, Hickman told Leopold he should look into mefloquine. "It set me on a path to investigate this drug," Leopold recalled. "It turned out to be this incredible, strange story that to this day remains a mystery." A mystery, it should be added, that remains so thanks to military censors and media spin artists—and a national security press with no stomach for compelling the Pentagon to account for its actions.

In 2015, Hickman wrote about what he witnessed at Guantanamo Bay in a riveting book, *Murder at Camp Delta*— which also chronicled the media blackout of the story. Unsurprisingly, Hickman's book was also largely ignored by the press. Meanwhile, the hand of military spin artists could be seen at work on Amazon, where *Murder at Camp Delta* came under vitriolic attack. A reviewer identifying himself as James Crabtree blasted the book on its Amazon page. "The only good thing I can say about *Murder at Camp Delta* is that, having read many volumes about the facility, it is refreshing to find a fantasy book about Gitmo torture written by some-one other than a former detainee for a change," Crabtree wrote. Although he didn't mention it in his review, Crabtree is a former public affairs officer at Guantanamo Bay.

Fifteen years after the beginning of the war on terror, not a single US official, military officer, or CIA interrogator at Guantanamo Bay or any of the other post-9/11 detention centers around the globe has been convicted in connection with the torture or death of a detainee. The only people associated with America's global gulag to be tried and punished were eleven low-level soldiers who served at Iraq's notorious Abu Ghraib prison. Those higher up in the chain of command have enjoyed legal immunity because there is virtually no public pressure in the United States for these officials to be held accountable. The massive public indifference to these crimes stems from the fact that the corporate media has almost entirely accepted the national security complex's rationale for the endless state of emergency imposed by the government after 9/11. The normal rules and legal constraints no longer apply, the government told the world after 9/11. And the media, by and large, continues to let this authoritarian state of affairs go unchallenged.

In fact, the only CIA officer even remotely connected to the agency's torture program to have so far faced justice is former CIA officer John Kiriakou, who spent two years in a federal prison in Pennsylvania for leaking classified information to a reporter. "I didn't think I was saying anything particularly controversial, but it turned out I was the first CIA official to ever acknowledge the fact that we were torturing prisoners," Kiriakou told me shortly after his release. Kiriakou's crime was not participating in waterboarding, but *exposing* it. This is the upside-down world that America's major press institutions have allowed to become entrenched in Washington, by refusing to challenge the national security state's Orwellian mentality. War Is Peace. Freedom Is Slavery. Ignorance Is Strength.

Chapter Six

Operation Tinseltown

———

A s we have seen, the CIA and the rest of America's vast shadow empire have been manipulating the press for as long as these secretive agencies have existed. But the clandestine effort to control public thought does not stop there. The CIA also makes a major effort to insert itself into our dream life.

It wasn't until the mid-1990s that the CIA formally hired an entertainment industry liaison and began openly courting favorable treatment in films and television, but the agency has been covertly working with Hollywood since its inception in 1947. As part of its lavishly budgeted, global propaganda campaign during the Cold War, the CIA secretly funded the production of the 1951 animated feature, *Animal Farm*, based on George Orwell's anti-communist parable, and selected producer Louis de Rochemont to oversee the film. (CIA officer Howard Hunt, later of Watergate fame, was tasked with purchasing rights to the book from Orwell's widow.) The

CIA made sure that the animated version of Orwell's story left out the late author's sour sentiments about the capitalist system, focusing its critique entirely on the grim aspects of communism. A few years later, the CIA arranged for the ending of Orwell's other classic novel, *1984*, to be changed in the 1956 film adaptation, with the protagonist heroically resisting attempts to brainwash him and rising up to challenge Big Brother's totalitarian system—rather than coming to love it, as in the book.

In her definitive book on the subject, *The Cultural Cold War: The CIA and the World of Arts and Letters*, British historian Frances Stonor Saunders cites a particularly egregious example of the CIA's early meddling in Hollywood concerning the 1958 film adaptation of Graham Greene's *The Quiet American*. In Greene's novel, which is set in French colonial Vietnam, the story is told from the perspective of British foreign correspondent Thomas Fowler, a sad but basically decent man enraptured by the virginal Phuong, his love interest. Fowler's would-be romance is stymied by Alden Pyle, a naïve-seeming American who—with his ardent good intentions—not only ends up crushing the dreams of his British friend, but also wreaking political havoc in Saigon. Greene—a one-time British secret agent who was no fan of Western colonialism or emerging American imperialism—made Pyle, who is revealed to be a CIA agent, into a symbol of the blundering arrogance that would soon enmesh the United States in its Southeast Asia nightmare.

When the CIA got wind that writer-director Joseph Mankiewicz was adapting *The Quiet American*, the agency moved swiftly to give the film a more positive spin. Edward Lansdale—a legendary CIA adventurer in the Far East and widely (although erroneously) believed to be the inspiration for Pyle's character—talked Mankiewicz into flipping the good- and bad-guy roles. Thus, in the film, the hero becomes Pyle, who is no longer the destructive innocent who sets off bombs in Saigon to discredit the anti-colonial rebels; and Fowler becomes a soft-on-communism stooge. A disgusted Greene denounced it as nothing more than a "propaganda film for America."

Based on what little reliable information has been published about the CIA and Hollywood, the agency's covert manipulation of the entertainment industry appears to have markedly decreased during the next two decades. In the 1970s, following the Watergate scandal and shocking congressional revelations about the CIA, a Hollywood backlash against the spy agency even took shape. A series of anti-authority thrillers, including classic conspiracy films like Francis Ford Coppola's *The Conversation* and Alan Pakula's *The Parallax View* (both released in 1974) and Sydney Pollack's *Three Days of the Condor* (1975), depicted the national security state as a malevolent force, with *Condor,* starring Robert Redford as a CIA whistle-blower, taking specific aim at the agency as an institution capable of killing anyone who gets in its way, even its own agents. For the first time since the spy agency's inception, its dark behavior had finally backfired, at least on screen.

In the 1980s, with the Reagan counterrevolution and subsequent escalation of Cold War tensions, Hollywood became more forgiving toward the national security state, despite occasional, if poorly marketed, exceptions like Costa-Gavras' *Missing* (1982), Roger Spottiswoode's *Under Fire* (1983), and Oliver Stone's passionate critique of Reagan's dirty war in Central America, *Salvador (1986),* which Stone was only able to get into theaters thanks to the box-office success of *Platoon*. Movies glorifying American militarism were more typical of the era, such as *Top Gun* and *Heartbreak Ridge* (1986), while writer-director John Milius' lunatic tale of a Cuban-Russian sneak attack on the American heartland, *Red Dawn* (1984), seemed to be readying Americans for an existential show-down with the global communist menace.

Perhaps the most bizarre interaction of Hollywood and the national security state in the 1980s involved a movie that never got made. In late 1986, amid high-profile hearings over the Iran-contra scandal, two competing efforts emerged to secure the film rights from key individuals who were involved with Oliver North's secret operation, including Eugene Hasenfus, the CIA-employed air cargo handler whose shoot-down and capture by the Sandinistas set off the scandal. One film group was led by ex-CIA officer Frank Snepp. After leaving the agency, Snepp wrote *Decent Interval*, a 1977 memoir about the ignominious US retreat from Saigon during which many Vietnamese who had collaborated with America were abandoned to their fate. An infuriated CIA responded by suing Snepp, and succeeded in confiscating his $300,000 in royalties. When news spread that the former CIA bad boy was going to shoot the Hasenfus story, the folks at Langley were clearly not pleased. Soon a more shadowy, rival group of filmmakers emerged to compete with the CIA critic.

This group was led by Larry Spivey, who was described in a 1987 *New York Times* article as a former navy counter-insurgency specialist. "Mr. Spivey says he is now a freelance movie producer," the *Times* observed. "But his company is not listed with any of the standard Hollywood unions or film production organizations, and the phone number he gives out elicits only a loud electronic buzz." In an interview with the *Times*, Spivey denied that "his relationship with Colonel North, who he says he met at a briefing on Nicaragua in the Old Executive Office Building," had any "bearing on the film project."

Snepp, who, as a producer for ABC's *World News Tonight,* had been covering the Iran-contra scandal, became involved with the Hasenfus project after telling his friend, actor Marlon Brando, that Hasenfus was an old colleague of his. "I had known Hasenfus well in Vietnam," Snepp recalled. "He was a baggage kicker there, just like in Iran-contra." At Brando's request, Snepp flew from Los Angeles to Wisconsin to meet Hasenfus, and returned with him to Brando's Mulholland Drive mansion, where the actor was waiting for them in a kimono. Halfway through their meeting, however, Hasenfus started "acting smug," according to Snepp, and mentioned that Spivey was offering him twice as much cash for his life rights than Brando had just offered. "I got suspicious that this was an Oliver North operation and that somebody in the White House was doing this," Snepp recalled. After checking with his sources in Vice President George H. W. Bush's office, Snepp confirmed that North was indeed trying to sabotage the Snepp-Brando movie project. In the end, his enemies in Washington succeeded, said Snepp. "Hasenfus finally clammed up because the national security community and Ollie North had Spivey as a friend, and he had all the money, so there was no movie. That was another way the public got played."

* * *

During the Clinton presidency, the CIA took its Hollywood strategy to a new level—trying to take more control of its own mythmaking. In 1996, the CIA hired one of its veteran clandestine officers, Chase Brandon, to work directly with Hollywood studios and production companies to upgrade its image. "We've always been portrayed erroneously as evil and Machiavellian," Brandon later told the *Guardian.* "It took us a long time to support projects that portray us in the light we want to be seen in."

The flag-waving Tom Clancy franchise became a centerpiece of CIA propaganda in the 1990s, with a succession of actors (Alec Baldwin, Harrison Ford, and finally Ben Affleck) starring in films like *Patriot Games, Clear and Present Danger*, and *The Sum of All Fears*, which pit the daring agent Jack Ryan against an array of enemies—from terrorists to South American drug lords to nuclear-armed white supremacists.

The long relationship between Affleck, a prominent Hollywood liberal, and Langley seems particularly perplexing. But the mutual admiration has paid off handsomely for all concerned. According to the *Guardian*, during the production of *The Sum of all Fears*, the 2002 Clancy thriller starring Affleck, "the agency was happy to bring its makers to Langley for a personal tour of headquarters, and to offer [the star] access to agency analysts. When filming began, [CIA liaison] Brandon was on set to advise."

The CIA's man in Hollywood was also a frequent presence on the set of *Alias*, the TV espionage series starring Affleck's then-wife, Jennifer Garner. The series, which debuted in September 2001, reflected the pervasive paranoia of the post-9/11 era—that climate of permanent anxiety so beloved by national security agencies. Created by Hollywood powerhouse J. J. Abrams, who would go on to reboot the *Star Trek* and *Star Wars* franchises, the show featured Garner as Sydney Bristow, a CIA undercover agent who infiltrated a global conspiracy.

In March 2004, the CIA announced that Garner—reflecting the growing merger between Langley and Hollywood—had filmed a recruitment video for the agency. "The video emphasizes the CIA's mission, and its need for people with diverse backgrounds and foreign language skills," the agency's press release stated. "Ms. Garner was excited to participate in the video after being asked by the Office of Public Affairs. The CIA's Film Industry Liaison worked with the writers of *Alias* during the first season to educate them on fundamental tradecraft. Although the show *Alias* is fictional, the character Jennifer Garner plays embodies the integrity, patriotism, and intelligence the CIA looks for in its officers."

Another TV show the CIA tasked Brandon to chaperone was *The Agency*, a CBS dramatic series showcasing American spy heroics. Weirdly, the series' September 2001 premiere (which had been filmed before 9/11) featured a plot by Osama bin Laden against Western targets, and it had to be delayed when reality trumped the script-writers. Since in real life the agency had failed to protect America from the 9/11 attacks, Langley understandably found the subject of bin Laden too sensitive to broach that month. The episode that replaced the original premiere featuring bin Laden had its own strange backstory, rewriting one of the most notorious chapters in CIA history. In *The Agency's* version, the CIA actually tries to stop an assassination plot against Fidel Castro—a plotline that the Cuban leader undoubtedly found amusing as would, for that matter, anyone else who recalled the spy outfit's relentless campaign to knock off Fidel over the years, using everything from a bazooka to a poisoned wetsuit.

As Hollywood became increasingly embedded with Langley following 9/11, CIA employees often saw their public affairs colleagues giving various celebrities personalized tours of the headquarters. "I can't tell you how many times this happened," recalled former CIA officer John Kiriakou. He would bump into a parade of Hollywood types, including Harrison Ford and Ben Affleck. *Why are these guys allowed to walk around a top-secret facility?* he wondered, with a rising sense of irritation. "Because he's going to be playing a CIA guy in a movie? That's the criteria now? You just have to be a friend of the agency and you can come in and walk around? In the meantime, people who are undercover are having to walk through the halls with their hands over their faces because these people aren't cleared. It's insane."

Langley's investment in Ben Affleck, and vice versa, paid handsome dividends with the hugely popular, if factually challenged, 2012 film *Argo*, directed by Affleck, who also starred as CIA makeup artist Tony Mendez. Based on a 2007 *Wired* magazine article by Joshuah Bearman, *Argo* told the [sort of] true story of how the CIA rescued several American hostages in Tehran, with the help of Mendez, who set up a fake Hollywood production company and was pretending to shoot a science fiction fantasy film in Iran. According to Richard Klein, a consultant who helps connect Hollywood studios with the CIA and other government agencies, *Argo* was the first movie to get permission to film inside Langley headquarters in fifteen years. When the crew arrived at the gate, they were told that nobody could bring electronics into the building. After everyone insisted they'd left all their phones and other gadgets behind, a security guard told them to check again. "Everyone says, 'Nope, no phones,'" Klein recalled. This time, the guard read aloud the make and model of the unaccounted phone. "Someone sheepishly 'fessed up to it," he said. "It was in a toolbox or something; they brought it out to the parking lot, left it there, and came back in."

Argo took many liberties with the truth, all of them geared to make Langley and Hollywood appear more heroic. For example, the significant role played by the Canadian embassy in helping the hostages escape was left out for storytelling purposes. And despite the film's dramatic conclusion, there were no gun-toting Iranian Revolutionary Guardsmen racing in jeeps down the runway after a jet plane full of fleeing Americans. But the movie won over audiences with its entertaining tale of a real-life *Mission Impossible*-style caper, while featuring the CIA in the most glowing, heroic light. In fact, *Argo*—which won three Academy Awards including Best Picture, and reaped over $230 million at the box office— arguably ranks as the agency's most successful propaganda coup in Hollywood.

"That was a grand slam," observed former CIA officer Robert Baer, whose memoir *See No Evil* inspired its own cinematic tale of foreign intrigue, the critically acclaimed 2005 film *Syriana*, with George Clooney starring as a fictional CIA officer partly based on Baer. But, Baer added, "*Argo* had nothing to do with reality. Anybody involved in that operation knows that. The unit Mendez worked for is fictional. He was a makeup guy. He made the first mustache I used. They aren't supposed to last a long time, so they don't remember your face." When people ask Baer what he thinks is the best film made about the CIA, he tells them to watch HBO's *The Wire*. "It's the same mindless bureaucracy and politics and ambition," he explained. "All the other crap you run into in a police department, you run into in intelligence."

Baer's career as a Hollywood consultant began after famed investigative reporter Seymour Hersh talked up *See No Evil* prior to publication. "The people at Warner Brothers said, 'This is what we want—a movie on intelligence and oil.' I don't think anybody read the whole book, they just locked [director Steven] Soderbergh in an office and had him read twenty pages." After Soderbergh purchased the rights to the book, Baer and screenwriter Stephen Gaghan flew to Beirut, Damascus, Syria, and Dubai. "We met some Syrian people I knew and I introduced them to one of my ex-bosses who had gotten into contracting after the CIA," Baer recalled. "Soderbergh and Gaghan used all these pieces from those trips, so the film has very little to do with *See No Evil.*"

Syriana emerged as a far more complex film than *Argo*, exploring the murky intersection of the oil industry, CIA intrigue, and Islamic radicalism. Although Baer didn't write the script, he suspects the CIA "couldn't have been too happy about the movie," given that the agency has banned his book from its bookstore at Langley. "I take it as a badge of honor," Baer said. "My book has turned into a recruiting tool for the CIA, to their horror, because people think they can join the agency, then just go wing it and write a book and make a movie."

* * *

Although its main character, Carrie Mathison (Claire Danes), is a bipolar CIA officer who must take medication to keep from suffering mental breakdowns and who frequently violates all kinds of protocols—even sleeping with the targets of her investigation—the Showtime television drama *Homeland* has become a favorite at CIA headquarters. Equally bedazzled is US Department of Homeland Security Director Jeh Johnson, who took a break from authorizing drone strikes to dine at a trendy spot in Manhattan's SoHo district with Danes, in a creepy publicity stunt staged by the *New York Times*. "Homeland Times Two," as the newspaper headlined the story. *Get it?* "More people have learned about targeted lethal killing from Claire than me," gushed fanboy Johnson.

"There is an appreciation for the show [in national security circles]," confirmed Alex Gansa, *Homeland*'s co-creator. "We really did not hear any criticism officially or in a back channel way about the show or the character [from the

CIA]." Even the psychologically troubled character played by Danes does not seem to ruffle feathers at the agency. "Are there bipolar people at Langley?" he asks. "Probably. Are they running sensitive operations? Who knows? Maybe, I'd like to know. I would be curious to see what effect *Homeland* might have on recruitment and whether there is more interest in becoming an intelligence officer."

The original idea for *Homeland* came from an Israeli television series called *Hatufim*, or *Prisoners of War*, which depicted Israeli soldiers returning from years in captivity, a classic homecoming yarn as old as Homer's *The Odyssey*. But over several seasons, *Homeland* has become a platform for Gansa to explore all the most compelling and controversial aspects of the war on terror from a reliably pro-CIA point of view. "We do not pull punches," Gansa insisted. "We are critical of our protagonist and the goals her superiors task her with. We try in a vigorous way to show both sides and not be polemic."

Gansa said the show has never filmed inside Langley headquarters, but he and several actors from the show were invited to spend the day there. "We sat across the desk from twenty or thirty intelligence officers." At one point, CIA Director John Brennan made an appearance. "It became apparent quite quickly there are parallels between actors and intelligence officers," Gansa observed. "They are almost always playing a role. If they are there under official cover at an embassy, or they are meeting people after work and seducing them in some way, in effect they are acting."

While visiting CIA headquarters, Mandy Patinkin, who plays the role of Mathison's boss—Saul Berenson, chief of Middle East operations—was allowed to visit Brennan's office. "Then a very funny thing happened," recalled Gansa. "They separated the people who had been born in the United

States and those where were not." This group included Gansa himself, who was born in the Philippines, as well as British actor Damien Lewis, and Brazilian-American actress Morena Baccarin. "We were not allowed in that part of the building where you could see an actual undercover person. We weren't even allowed where the gift shop was because you could possibly see into the cafeteria. We were feeling very left out."

There is a revolving door between the CIA and Hollywood regarding shows like *Homeland*. After two seasons, as *Homeland*'s focus shifted overseas and began to hew more closely to real events, Gansa offered a consulting job to former CIA deputy director John MacGaffin, whose cousin, Henry Bromell, was one of the show's original writers and whose father, Leon, had served as a CIA officer in Cairo, Teheran, and Kuwait. A successful screenwriter for *Homicide* and *Northern Exposure*, among others, Bromell died of a heart attack in 2013. "Henry would call me occasionally when he was doing things, including the first part of *Homeland*," MacGaffin recalled. "I'd give him clear and candid answers, and realized he was giving them to all the writers. At his funeral, I met Alex Gansa and he introduced me to all the writers. They told me that whenever they got stuck [on a story problem], they would say, 'Let's talk to John MacGaffin.' I'm glad I didn't know or I would have failed all my polygraph tests."

Every year since he's been attached to *Homeland*, MacGaffin said, Gansa, Danes, Patinkin, and several of the show's writers visit him in Washington, D.C. "For three days, nine or ten hours a day, I run people through them who are retired from the agency and the FBI and the State Department," he says. "I brought an array of people who can talk, and told them there is no money in this for you guys, but if you believe in what we do as an agency, here's a chance to spend some time working on the best and most-watched story on our old business. Every one of them has said that's worth doing."

MacGaffin recalls telling his friend David Ignatius—the *Washington Post* columnist and spy novelist with friendly ties to the CIA from his days covering the Lebanese civil war—that he was working on the show. "I didn't know you were doing this," Ignatius told him. "Now I know why I like the show so much."

It's a cozy culture of collaboration. And while the involvement of ex-spooks like MacGaffin and his old colleagues inevitably gives the show a realistic tone and accurate sense of spycraft, this verisimilitude comes with a price. For it also bolsters an already inherently pro-agency slant to the espionage series. For example, in the show's fifth season, which was filmed on location in Germany, a character clearly based on Snowden's journalistic partner Laura Poitras (she was even named "Laura" in the show) is portrayed as so zealously committed to the principle of freedom of information and the "hacktivist" underground that she puts Berlin at serious risk of a nerve gas attack by Islamic terrorists. And while *Homeland's* CIA protagonists are portrayed as flawed, and often tormented, heroes, the bottom line is they are heroes. Their Islamic militant antagonists, on the other hand, are generally filmed in conspiratorial shadows, and are portrayed as fanatics whose souls have become twisted by years of struggle against the West. The legitimate grievances that the Muslim populations of the Middle East might have, following decades of Western imperialism, exploitation, and violence are barely touched on.

Consultants who help Hollywood producers tackle espionage stories say the dream factory usually gets the intelligence world wrong for all the right reasons—the industry is in the entertainment business, after all, and facts should never get in the way of a good story. Generally speaking, as long as movies stick to fiction, the CIA claims it doesn't care how it is depicted. Thus, a franchise like the *Mission Impossible* series—the most recent installment of which, *Rogue Nation*, portrays the agency as a feckless bureaucracy while its shadowy subcontractor, the Impossible Mission Force, repeatedly saves the world by operating outside the law—doesn't even register a blip on Langley's radar screen. Generally speaking, intelligence consultants, especially former members of spy agencies, try not to attach themselves to projects that might seriously compromise the public image of their former employers. While providing technical advice for minor plot points and set decorations for favorable or neutral projects, they also seek to ensure that nothing portrayed in the film might inadvertently upset the CIA or other agencies.

"The *Bourne* movies they cringe about mostly because of how disconnected from reality they are," said consultant Richard Klein, referring to one particular scene in which the protagonist is able to read the combination of a safe being opened inside a CIA safe house by spying through a window from across the street. "That one absolutely stood out as hysterical. In general, such films show the CIA like a facility on the Google campus, but the reality is these are government office buildings with government furniture that is chipped and stained, wood with round edges." Klein tried to help capture that aesthetic when he consulted on the 2012 Denzel Washington thriller *Safe House*. "Originally, in the art department sketches, [the CIA safe house] looked like a high-end college dorm room and ignored the functionality of what the agency needs these places for. The reality is these guys work in cramped conditions and uncomfortable places, so to show it correctly is much appreciated."

* * *

Before *Homeland*, Alex Gansa worked as writer on the seventh and eighth seasons of the Fox television show, *24*, the series that sparked a fiery debate over the way that it justified torture as a tool to fight terrorism. It is difficult to conceive of a more blatantly manipulative TV show than *24* in the post-9/11 era, with its constant siege of ruthless enemies, countdown clock imagery, and pulse-pounding soundtrack, all serving to ratchet up the American people's anxiety level and our willingness to accept extreme security measures in the name of public safety.

Gansa acknowledged that the behavior of the show's main character, agent Jack Bauer (Kiefer Sutherland) of the "Counter Terrorist Unit," was intended to be a lightning rod for controversy. "Jack tortured people and it worked, in the context of a ticking time bomb situation—and, of course in real life, that never happens. The show did come under a lot of criticism for that. What's interesting is that because of *24*, popular culture became the talking point that stirred the debate."

But Gansa stopped short of taking any responsibility for helping create a cultural climate in which CIA extraordinary rendition, black sites, and enhanced interrogation became part of the acceptable new norm during the Bush-Cheney years. In some ways, *24*—which enjoyed a long, successful run, from 2001 to 2010—segued perfectly into *Homeland*. Though Gansa's Showtime series is much more dramatically complex than the Fox thriller, there is the same underlying theme that our nation's guardians must be willing to take drastic action—even if there is collateral damage, even if innocent people suffer, even if it corrupts these security agents' own souls. In a way, Claire Danes' Carrie Mathison is simply a more sophisticated version of Sutherland's Jack Bauer.

Hollywood gave Langley another propaganda gift in the growing debate over torture when the film *Zero Dark Thirty* was released in 2012. The film reunited director Kathryn Bigelow and screenwriter Mark Boal, the creative team behind *The Hurt Locker*, a gritty depiction of a US Army bomb disposal unit in Iraq which won the 2009 Academy Award for Best Picture. Bigelow and Boal tried to bring the same sense of gripping reality to their new project, which purported to tell the "story of history's greatest manhunt for the world's most dangerous man," Osama bin Laden. When President Obama announced on May 1, 2011, that an elite team of US Navy SEALs had just killed bin Laden at a compound in the Pakistani city of Abbottabad, the CIA was already helping Boal with a script involving bin Laden's escape from the Tora Bora cave complex in Afghanistan. Now that he had a concrete ending to the bin Laden tale, Boal started rewriting. He and Bigelow also began pressing CIA and Pentagon officials for as much access as possible to people involved in hunting and killing bin Laden. In other words, the makers of *Zero Dark Thirty* were deeply embedded in the US security world from the very beginning.

According to a report by the Defense Department's inspector general, then-CIA Director Leon Panetta seemed to have stardust in his eyes over the prospect of a Hollywood version of the search for bin Laden. The CIA chief hoped that Al Pacino would play him in the movie. (The role went instead to *Sopranos* star James Gandolfini.) Panetta allowed screenwriter Boal to attend a June 2011 meeting at Langley that was closed to the press and attended by all the major players in the operation. The CIA chief also gave Boal names of people whose role in the mission was still secret, and shared other classified information with the filmmakers.

A FOIA request about the film filed by Judicial Watch, a conservative watchdog group, turned up a series of emails between the filmmakers and Langley that further demonstrated how eager the CIA was to support the project. On June 7, 2011, CIA spokesperson Marie E. Harf argued that both the agency and Pentagon should back the Boal/Bigelow film over competing projects. "I know we don't pick favorites but it makes sense to get behind a winning horse," she wrote. "Mark and Kathryn's movie is going to be the first and the biggest. It's got the most money behind it, and two Oscar winners on board."

Several weeks later, on July 20, Boal emailed then-CIA Director of Public Affairs George Little and thanked him for "pulling for him," which he was certain had made "all the difference." Little's response made no attempt to hide the agency's pleasure. "I can't tell you how excited we all are," he wrote. "PS—I want you to know how good I've been not mentioning the premiere tickets."

As the filmmakers wrapped up pre-production work, they sent numerous emails to Langley asking for help on even the minutest of details, including the floor plan of the Abbottabad compound. "Ok, I checked with our folks, and that floor plan matches with what we have," a spokesperson responded. "It looks legit to us."

That accomplished, Boal and Bigelow requested even more information about the building. "Would you mind looking into getting us some of the third-floor specs," they asked in one email. "We will be building a full scale replica of the house. Including the inhabitants of the animal pen!"

Records show that the CIA responded immediately with a promise to help. "Ha! Of course I don't mind!" a spokesperson wrote. "I'll work on that tomorrow."

The partnership between Langley and the *Zero Dark Thirty* filmmakers proved so tight that national security reporters felt slighted. "A lot of other people who covered the beat like I did in that search for bin Laden—we didn't get close to that kind of cooperation from the agency on telling the inside story," long-time *Washington Post* intelligence reporter Greg Miller later told PBS's *Frontline*.

In the end, the CIA's energetic cooperation with Boal and Bigelow paid off enormously, with *Zero Dark Thirty* serving as the most effective piece of propaganda for the agency's torture program since *24*. The film made the case that bin Laden's capture would not have been possible without information that was extracted under torture. The filmmakers might have taken great pains to portray the smallest details of bin Laden's compound accurately. But on this fundamental issue, they blatantly violated the truth.

After the film was released in December 2012, it came under sharp attack by Senator Dianne Feinstein, who chaired the Senate intelligence committee's torture investigation, and Senator John McCain, himself a torture victim at the hands of the North Vietnamese. As the Senate committee determined, CIA interrogators gained no useful information by torturing their victims, either regarding bin Laden's whereabouts or any other significant security issue. McCain's rejection of the film's CIA-friendly premise was particularly persuasive: "I know from personal experience that the abuse of prisoners will produce more bad than good intelligence. . . . Acting without conscience isn't necessary; it isn't even helpful in fighting this strange and long war we're fighting."

Feinstein, who shared McCain's convictions about torture, was outraged by *Zero Dark Thirty*, walking out of a special screening arranged for her just fifteen or twenty minutes into the film. "I couldn't handle it," she explained. "Because it is so false."

In September 2015, *Vice* reporter Jason Leopold published a story based on the CIA's own Inspector General report, titled "Potential Ethics Violations Involving Film Producers," which revealed even more embarrassing details about the CIA's cozy relationship with Boal and Bigelow. As it turned out, the filmmakers had wined and dined agency officials in Hollywood and at a hotel near CIA headquarters, routinely racking up thousand-dollar restaurant bills. At one point, the Inspector General report stated a female CIA officer mentioned liking the fashion designer Prada. Boal responded by saying "he knew the designer personally and offered her tickets to a Prada fashion show." The same officer later dined with the filmmakers at the Ritz Carlton hotel in Washington, D.C's, upscale Georgetown neighborhood, where as a thank-you gift, Bigelow, who had just returned from filming a commercial in Tahiti, gave her a pair of "black Tahitian pearl earrings." (The officer gave the jewelry to Langley to be appraised, and thus learned they were fake.) A bottle of tequila that Boal gave another officer, which was supposedly worth "several hundred dollars," could be bought for $100. None of the officers kept the gifts and the report cleared them of any wrongdoing.

Even *Homeland* creator Gansa and the show's ex-CIA consultant MacGaffin were unnerved by the liberties with the truth taken by Boal and Bigelow regarding CIA torture. Gansa said the *Zero Dark Thirty* controversy illustrates the dangers of working with agency consultants who may have their own agendas. "I was so upset about that movie," Gansa said. "Clearly Mark and Kathryn did research but they listened to a consultant who felt that torture clearly worked and led to the capture of Osama bin Laden. Many people would dispute that, so to represent that as the truth and put that out there to millions of people? You don't take one person's word as gospel and present it as factual."

MacGaffin believes that the CIA's efforts to hoodwink the public by spinning the *Zero Dark Thirty* filmmakers betray a guilty conscience about the agency's use of torture. "I think about what decisions I would have made if I was there," MacGaffin adds, referring specifically to the chain of command that signed off on waterboarding and other "enhanced interrogation methods" used on CIA detainees. "At the time, everyone 'knew' that [captured terrorists like] Abu Zubaydah absolutely 'knew' about other attacks. We were 'absolutely certain.' I think I too would have probably said, 'We have got to [use torture].' But I would hope after a month I would have said, 'Why are we still doing this?'"

* * *

"Of course it's crap," said ex-CIA officer Baer of *Zero Dark Thirty*. "And nobody with any knowledge of the movie industry should be surprised," said the veteran spook. After all, Hollywood routinely turns out thrilling escapades featuring spies and soldiers that are utter nonsense. "Like *Lone Survivor*," he added. In the view of some Navy SEALs who are familiar with the 2005 battle against the Afghan Taliban that is depicted in the film, its real-life protagonist, Marcus Lutrell, was no hero. Former CIA officer, author, and CNN consultant Robert Baer has even charged that "Lutrell went and hid. The SEALs hate that guy."

Nonetheless, the 2013 action film starring Mark Wahlberg, which was based on Lutrell's book of the same name and written and directed by Peter Berg, won the full cooperation of the Pentagon after the filmmakers submitted the script for military approval. In fact, the Pentagon was so happy with *Lone Survivor* that it provided Berg and his team with five SEALs—three retired and two active—as consultants. Apparently, the military had no problem whatsoever with the gross distortions of fact that characterized Lutrell's book as well as the movie, since they made the ill-fated SEAL team seem even more heroic.

Although Lutrell wrote in his after-action report that his SEAL team had been wiped out by twenty to thirty Taliban fighters, the actual number of enemy combatants was more likely closer to one dozen fighters, armed with a heavy machine gun. In his book, Lutrell upped the number even higher, to between 140 to 200 fighters, while the filmmakers went even more Fort Apache, depicting hundreds of Taliban warriors surrounding the doomed American heroes. In the movie, Lutrell is nearly beheaded by a Taliban commander before being rescued by a helicopter gunship crew, braving intense enemy fire to swoop him to safety. In real life, Afghan villagers protected Lutrell from the Taliban until he could be airlifted to a hospital; there was no climactic firefight.

In terms of box-office success, no Hollywood film has succeeded in mythologizing the war against terror as effectively as Clint Eastwood's masterfully directed *American Sniper*, based on the bestselling memoir by Chris Kyle, who—with more than 160 confirmed kills in the Iraq War—is the most lethal sniper in US military history. Unsurprisingly, Eastwood gave the hero treatment to Kyle (played by Bradley Cooper), a man who as an expert assassin certainly had more than his share of demons. The director chose to leave out Kyle's own tragic ending, though some might consider it poetic. The sniper was gunned down on a Texas shooting range in February 2013 by a mentally ill veteran.

"Everyone thought [Kyle] was nuts [in real life]," Baer remarked, adding that Hollywood's whitewashing of the story took nobody in the intelligence community, himself included, by surprise. "It's all bullshit, but it doesn't matter in Hollywood. If you tell them that's not how it works, they look at you like you've lost your mind." Clearly, Eastwood's clean-up job on Kyle worked at the box office, where the film generated $500 million worldwide. But Hollywood liberals, guilt-stricken over a blockbuster that celebrated a homicidal hero of an illegal war, made sure that Eastwood, Cooper, and the film itself were snubbed at Oscar time.

Hollywood writer and director Peter Landesman agreed that some filmmakers are too easily dazzled by consultants filled with swashbuckling tales from their clandestine lives. Landesman, who worked as a foreign correspondent in Pakistan after 9/11 and wrote national security stories for the *New York Times* magazine, was equipped with a better bullshit meter than most filmmakers by the time he got to Hollywood. "I have had a number of dealings with the CIA, both as a journalist and as a screenwriter," he said. "I quickly learned that I could never, ever, take what any officer or operative says at face value. They are hardwired to deflect, even off the record. Also, as underpaid and overworked civil servants, they frequently try to cash in on their experience. Almost always, they inflate their role and their own involvement."

Landesman wrote the script for the 2014 film about the late investigative journalist Gary Webb, *Kill the Messenger*, which—full disclosure alert—was based both on Webb's book *Dark Alliance* and my 2006 book about Webb that shares the film's title. Given the harsh light that Webb's story placed on both the CIA and the nation's three most power-ful newspapers, it was something of a miracle that *Kill the Messenger* somehow made it to the screen. Universal Pictures first optioned the film rights to my book in 2008, but dropped the project after another political/espionage/media thriller, *State of Play* (starring, of course, Ben Affleck, with Russell Crowe), flopped at the box office the following year. *Kill the Messenger* finally was picked up by Focus Features, and director Michael Cuesta succeeded in making a gripping film from Landesman's script, starring Jeremy Renner as Webb.

The scenes depicting how Webb was crushed by editors at the CIA-friendly *New York Times, Washington Post,* and *Los Angeles Times*—as well as his own paper, the *San Jose Mercury News*—rank as among the most powerful indict-ments of the press in screen history (and since I had little to do with the making of the film, I can state this with objectiv-ity). Unfortunately, prior to its release in October 2014, *Kill the Messenger* became an orphaned project when the studio went through a management change and the incoming exec-utives chose to use the bulk of the film's massive marketing budget to launch their pet project, the hugely successful *The Theory of Everything.* Despite glowing reviews for Renner's performance, the lack of marketing or advertising doomed *Kill the Messenger* to fare poorly at the box office.

Needless to say, the CIA was happy to see the movie quickly disappear. Langley had taken note as *Kill the Messenger* worked its way through the development and pro-duction process in Hollywood, and an agency spokesperson acknowledged to me that he attended a screening of the film at the National Press Club in Washington, D.C., sitting next to a *New York Times* reporter in the audience. Not surpris-ingly, neither of them liked the film.

Kill the Messenger stirred up all of the old anti-Webb animus in the corporate media. Just before the movie opened, Jeff Leen, the *Washington Post*'s managing editor for investigations, penned a stunningly hostile posthumous hit-piece titled "Gary Webb Was No Journalism Hero" in which he rehashed the paper's criticism of "Dark Alliance," and, playing movie critic, trashed the film. "As for *Kill the Messenger*, the best that can be said for the movie is that Jeremy Renner gives a spirited performance in a fantasy version of the story in which everyone is wrong but Gary Webb," Leen wrote. "It would take an article longer than this one to point out the many departures from what really happened."

Leen—who had been an investigative reporter for the *Miami Herald* during the 1980s, where he covered the Colombian cartels and their violent takeover of Caribbean cocaine smuggling routes—clearly bore a personal grudge against Webb, and had once even debated Webb about the CIA-drug connection in the late 1980s. Reporters like Leen—who had failed to expose this connection—seemed to make it their personal mission to keep defaming Webb, even if it meant digging up his grave to do so.

As the war on terror endlessly grinds on, and the surveillance state continues to insert itself into every aspect of our lives, it will be interesting to see whether Hollywood finally begins to take a more critical look at the national security complex. But, as we've seen, recent trends are not encouraging. With few exceptions, like *Kill the Messenger*—which was indifferently distributed and promoted—Hollywood has functioned as a propaganda factory, churning out jingoistic revenge-fantasy films, in which American audiences are allowed to exorcise their post-9/11 demons by watching the satisfying slaughter of countless onscreen jihadis. This never-ending parade of square-jawed secret agents and bearded, pumped-up commandos pitted against swarthy Muslim madmen straight out of central casting has been aided and abetted by a newly emboldened CIA all too happy to offer its "services" to Hollywood. In exchange for special guided tours at Langley and lunches with national security czars, Hollywood filmmakers have eagerly turned themselves into propagandists for perpetual war and apologists for crimes against humanity.

Chapter Seven

A Wilderness of Mirrors

T he summary execution of Osama bin Laden was the crowning achievement of President Barack Obama's two-term career as America's commander in chief. It has also given rise to the greatest mythmaking in America's war on terror—a war, in fact, that has been driven by myths from the very beginning. The hunting down of the most wanted man in the world was the result of masterful espionage work, according to this tale—which has been told in countless press accounts, books, and movies like *Zero Dark Thirty*. But the truth is not quite so heroic.

The basic facts of the bin Laden raid itself are mostly uncontested. At about half-past midnight on May 2, 2011, a pair of modified US Blackhawk helicopters equipped with the latest stealth technology began to descend over a walled-off compound in Abbottabad, a garrison town in the heart of Pakistan's military-industrial complex. Located just a mile away from an army school, the building had been watched around the clock for months by CIA drones circling unseen high above the city.

As the Blackhawks swooped down on bin Laden and his family, President Obama nervously monitored the operation from the White House Situation Room, accompanied by Vice President Joe Biden and several other top officials. Just as the first helicopter was about to touch down, air currents that had been whipped up by the helicopter's rotors and trapped by the eighteen-foot walls caused the aircraft to lose its lift. The helicopter's tail broke off on the wall and the aircraft spilled into the courtyard, landing on its side. Although neither the pilots nor the heavily armed members of the US Navy's elite SEAL Team Six were injured, the importance of the helicopter crash would only become apparent years later.

What happened next has been told countless times, in highly detailed and contradictory accounts, with competing assertions about whether a firefight or a massacre took place, and varying estimates offered regarding exactly how many shots were fired and who shot them. But the general consensus is that two dozen SEALs blasted their way into the main building and proceeded to shoot and kill five people, including bin Laden and one of his sons. Leaving the rest of the bodies where they fell, the SEALs hauled bin Laden's corpse out of the house, along with a "treasure trove" of documents and digital files.

After blowing up the disabled helicopter, several of the SEALs got back on the surviving Blackhawk, while the remainder boarded a pair of backup Chinook helicopters along with what was left of Osama bin Laden, and flew back to Afghanistan. After bin Laden's identity had been confirmed via DNA and other means, his body was flown to the aircraft carrier *USS Carl Vinson*, and within twenty-four hours, it had been tossed into the Arabian Sea, either out of respect for Islamic tradition, which dictates swift burial, or to prevent his grave from becoming a destination for tourists or sympathizers. President Obama delivered a formal announcement of bin Laden's death on the White House lawn. From there, the news quickly spread around the world, and crowds of young Americans surrounded the White House chanting "USA, USA, USA."

Killing Osama bin Laden represented the biggest victory, at least in propaganda terms, in America's decade-long war on terror. (As detailed in the previous chapter, it even led to a major motion picture.) But soon, the official story of the raid came under intense questioning. How had bin Laden managed to avoid being noticed by the Pakistani government for so long, even though he was living just blocks away from a military base in one of the most secure cities in the country? Why wasn't the master terrorist taken alive, to be put on trial before the world? Certainly there had to be more to the story, and just how much of the official tale was even true?

In spite of the lack of concrete evidence being offered to support the White House's version, the basic facts of the bin Laden raid remained unchallenged until May 10, 2015, when the *London Review of Books* published a front-page story about the kill operation by legendary investigative reporter Seymour Hersh. "It's been four years since a group of US Navy SEALs assassinated Osama bin Laden in a night raid on a high-walled compound in Abbottabad, Pakistan," his story began. "The killing was the high point of Obama's first term, and a major factor in his re-election. The White House still maintains that the mission was an all-American affair, and that the senior generals of Pakistan's army and Inter-Services Intelligence agency (ISI) were not told of the raid in advance. This is false, as are many other elements of the

Obama administration's account. The White House's story might have been written by Lewis Carroll."

To begin with, wrote Hersh, the labyrinthine story given by the administration of how the CIA had painstakingly tracked down bin Laden, finally tracing him to the Abbottabad compound, was all just an elaborate cover story. In reality, Hersh claimed, ISI—the Pakistani security agency—had been holding bin Laden under house arrest since 2006, keeping him imprisoned in the compound as an intelligence asset, perhaps saving him for some future purpose. At one point, an ISI officer seeking $25 million in reward money came to the CIA with bin Laden's whereabouts. After some debate, the Obama administration worked out a plan with ISI whereby the Americans would grab bin Laden, with the ISI ensuring that local forces wouldn't intervene, and remove him to just across the lawless border with Afghanistan, where he would then be executed. To save Pakistan's national honor, the world would be told that bin Laden had died in a firefight in the middle of no-man's-land, instead of being gunned down in the middle of a Pakistani military town. Presumably, the helicopter crash fouled up that cover story, and when Obama went public with news of the raid, Hersh wrote, he not only threw the Pakistani government under the bus, he turned the biggest victory in the war on terror into an even bigger lie.

The Obama White House and CIA were stung by the article, and it didn't take long for vehement denunciations of Hersh to erupt from official Washington. Unsurprisingly, it was Langley's faithful friend, the *Washington Post,* which was first to showcase the rebuttals. An unnamed CIA official informed the *Post* that Hersh's story "is utter nonsense," the paper reported the day after Hersh's story appeared. "White House spokesman Ned Price said it had 'too many inaccuracies and baseless assertions' to fact-check each one." The article also quoted CNN analyst Peter Bergen, one of the few Western journalists who had ever interviewed bin Laden, who called Hersh's story a "farrago of nonsense that is contravened by a multitude of eyewitness accounts, inconvenient facts, and simple common sense."

Continuing to pile on was *Washington Post* media critic Erik Wemple as he ripped into Hersh for basing his article on just two primary sources—a retired Pakistani general named Asad Durrani and an anonymous, high-ranking US official with unspecified "knowledge" about the raid. Wemple noted that the anonymous official alone accounted for no less than fifty-five separate statements of facts in Hersh's story. "There's always one guy who tells you the secret," Hersh told Wemple.

Two days after official Washington dumped on Hersh in its pages, the *Post* continued the barrage, noting that several veteran journalists were attacking Hersh's reporting, particularly his gruesome claim that bin Laden's bullet-riddled body hadn't been buried at sea but torn apart and scattered like chum out the window of a helicopter flying over the Hindu Kush. The newspaper quoted one anonymous investigative reporter who, while not adding much clarity to the story, certainly captured the froth of feelings swirling around it. "The story is so fucking awful, people can't fucking deal with it," the reporter exclaimed. "[Everyone's] going fucking crazy."

When a *Post* reporter asked the famously abrasive Hersh for a reply, he was subjected to a fusillade of f-bombs. "It's not my fault I have fucking sources most reporters don't have," Hersh shot back. "People are just fucking batshit about this." When pressed to explain why the story hadn't run in the *New Yorker* magazine, Hersh's journalistic home in recent years, Hersh said that editor David Remnick had refused to publish it as a feature-length article, although he had inexplicably offered to let him write it as a blog. Remnick is well known for his sense of caution—some might say timidity, which probably accounts for his long reign at the magazine. And, as *New York* magazine later pointed out, Hersh's piece directly contradicted the magazine's previous reporting on Abbottabad, all of which was, of course, edited by Remnick.

The attacks on Hersh grew increasingly snarky. Writing in *Politico*, the voice of Beltway conventional wisdom, media columnist Jack Shafer dismissed Hersh's piece as "a messy omelet of a piece," thus dodging the question of whether the story was in fact true. "By re-exploring the bin Laden oper-ation, Hersh has thrust himself into the phenomenological territories that Cold War spymaster James Jesus Angleton called a 'wilderness of mirrors.' In this clandestine world, truths are constructed, obliterated, and bent to serve their masters. Adversaries who would deceive abound in this place, and without a reliable map, a compass, a sense of direction, and maybe even a pedometer, even the most intrepid voy-ager (or journalist) can find himself lost. I'll volunteer to join a search party for Hersh—somebody I've long admired—if only somebody can tell me precisely where he is."

Amid the growing chorus of criticism, Hersh found him-self increasingly isolated. But certain aspects of his story rang true to some reporters who had been covering Pakistan since 9/11, including Carlotta Gall of the *New York Times,* who wrote that while she had heard that bin Laden's location had been handed to the United States by a Pakistani informer within days of the raid, "no one could or would corrobo-rate the claim." Two years later, when Gall was conducting research for a book, "a high-level member of the Pakistani intelligence service" told her "that the ISI had been hiding bin Laden and ran a desk specifically to handle him as an intelligence asset." Later, Gall continued, she learned that the CIA's "walk-in" source was a Pakistani Army brigadier and senior ISI officer who told the agency that bin Laden was under the control of the ISI. "I trusted my source," Gall wrote. "I did not speak with him, and his information came to me through a friend, but he was high enough in the intelligence apparatus to know what he was talking about. I was confident the information was true, but I held off publishing it. It was going to be extremely difficult to corroborate in the United States, not least because the informant was presumably in witness protection."

* * *

More than a year after Hersh's story dropped like a bomb on official Washington, no new evidence has emerged either backing up or refuting his claims—which in itself speaks volumes about the compromised nature of the national security press. Given the fact that, as Gall wrote, well-placed sources in Pakistani intelligence have confirmed the basic thrust of Hersh's story, why have so many powerful media outlets in the United States been unable to either advance the story or convincingly disprove it? Instead, national security reporters have simply circulated vague denials from White House officials and Langley spokespeople. When pressed to comment on the Hersh story during an interview for this book at Langley headquarters, a CIA spokesperson repeated the agency's flat denial, calling it "complete nonsense," and claiming, although without providing any facts, that Gall's follow-up story was "off-track." Meanwhile, the press preferred to keep taking potshots at Hersh's crabby and headstrong personality, rather than doing any further investigation into the bin Laden operation.

Ex-spook Bob Baer says he has mixed views about Hersh's story: "He had a shitty goddamn editor," but parts of the story still ring true for Baer. In his experience, the SEALs would never send dozens of operatives in several helicopters into a high-security city like Abbottabad without clearing it first with the Pakistanis. "A SEAL team doesn't get ahead of the pack, they have all sorts of backup right in the vicinity," said Baer. "Someone in Pakistan knew this raid was coming. I know Pakistan, and foreigners don't set up in a garrison town like Abbottabad and not come to someone's attention." *Especially the most wanted man in the world*. "I had some real problems with that [part of the official story]. . . . I talked to the SEALs and there are all kinds of holes in it."

National security reporters with a more independent streak than the Beltway press pack—like *Vice*'s Jason Leopold—also never bought the White House version of Abbottabad. On the night Obama announced bin Laden's death, Leopold joined numerous other reporters in a conference call organized by the White House.

"They started saying things that didn't make sense," Leopold recalled. "Their stories had holes and after the call was over, I called my editor and said, 'There is no way I am fucking reporting this, because we are going to have to issue a correction. I think this stuff is wrong.' It reminded me of how there was so much excitement among reporters after 9/11. Everyone was lapping up whatever the government said about what was happening, and re-reporting it."

According to Leopold, all the stories printed about the bin Laden raid by all the prominent national security reporters closely followed the script that had been laid out in the conference call. "Everybody reported as fact what they said," he says. "Sure enough, the story completely unraveled. Based on certain things I've learned over the years, for example, I absolutely believe there was a walk-in." In other words, Pakistani intelligence handed bin Laden over to the Americans. He was not tracked down as a result of masterful CIA sleuthing.

Despite whatever flaws there might be in Hersh's reporting, it now seems that his basic observation is true: namely, the biggest success story in America's war on terror is nothing more than a fairy tale concocted by government officials and disseminated by a salivating Washington press corps and Hollywood filmmakers.

Reached by telephone at his home office in Washington, D.C., Hersh insisted he had nothing new to add to the debate over his work. He refused to discuss how he reported his story and was hesitant to speculate about why it was so controversial. "Here's the problem," he said. "I just don't know. It doesn't matter what I expect or believe. I have this great belief that cable news would collapse completely if every reporter who goes on those shows takes away two words: 'I think.' I don't do those shows."

Hersh took strong issue with the notion that if the official bin Laden raid story really was a lie, the truth could not have been covered up, because too many people would have known what really happened. But intelligence agencies *do* know how to keep things secret, he said—that's their job. Hersh used the NSA's wiretapping scandal as an example: the agency is one of the largest in the US government, and yet many of its secrets were ultimately spilled by exactly one person, Edward Snowden, Hersh pointed out. "According to public figures there are thirty thousand employees at the NSA," Hersh elaborated. Assuming that only 10 percent of the NSA's staff knew the agency was illegally collecting data from American citizens, that would work out to three thousand people who might have been aware of what was happening. So even if you assume that only a sliver of the total workforce knew, that's still a lot of people who managed to keep their mouths shut.

"You don't think guys in the NSA or CIA can keep secrets?" Hersh asked before hanging up the phone. "Oh yes they can, baby."

Conclusion

The Wolf

Remote even by the standards of Pakistan's almost completely lawless Federally Administrated Tribal Areas, the Shawal Valley is surrounded by steep mountains whose snow-covered slopes descend into thick forests interspersed with boulder-strewn alpine rivers. The valley is also the final redoubt of al-Qaeda and Taliban fighters who fled Afghanistan after the US invasion and carpet bombing of Osama bin Laden's cave complex at Tora Bora. Numerous Pakistani military offensives have so far failed to dislodge the terrorists, although their ranks have been decimated, a handful of targets at a time, by hundreds of American drone strikes.

On January 15, 2015, the CIA carried out yet another drone strike in the Shawal Valley—but this one would prove particularly problematic for the Obama assassination program.

Obama administration officials tout its remote-controlled killing operation as surgical in its precision. But as the

123

Intercept would report a few months after this Shawal Valley strike, the US drone program has resulted in a shocking level of "collateral damage," with a stunning 90 percent of recent drone strike victims in Afghanistan found to be innocent, according to classified documents leaked to the investigative website.

In the weeks leading up to the Shawal Valley operation in January 2015, CIA-operated drones had filmed four men coming and going from the target zone. They appeared to be males of military service age, and the CIA suspected that they were al-Qaeda-affiliated fighters already approved for targeted assassination. Anonymous US officials later told the *New York Times* that the agency had analyzed so-called "pattern of life" evidence to determine that the compound was being used by terrorists. The CIA also said it had intercepted cell phone calls and had obtained other unspecified intelligence that the four men were "al-Qaeda operatives and possibly members of the Islamic Movement of Uzbekistan." On the basis of this pattern of evidence, as opposed to the firm identification of a specific suspect, the CIA authorized a so-called "signature" strike on the compound.

But the CIA soon realized something had gone awry when its analysts reviewed drone footage shot in the aftermath of the explosion. Six bodies, not four, were dragged from the rubble and quickly buried, as the *Times* reported in its April 23, 2015, article on the strike. Among the dead were two Western hostages: Warren Weinstein, an American humanitarian, and Giovanni Lo Porto, an Italian aid worker.

Lo Porto had traveled to Pakistan from his hometown of Palermo, Sicily, in 2010, to work with a Germany-based relief organization that was helping the country rebuild after massive flooding that year. Along with a German national, Bernd Muehlenbeck, he had been kidnapped by four armed men on January 19, 2012. When Muehlenbeck's captors released him in October 2014, he stated that he'd been separated from Lo Porto months earlier and had no idea of his whereabouts. Weinstein, the seventy-three-year-old director of the Northern Virginia–based international development company J. E. Austin and Associates, was in Pakistan to supervise his company's US-backed $11 million aid project in the tribal areas. Abducted during a pre-dawn raid at his house in Lahore on August 13, 2011, a gaunt-looking Weinstein had starred in several proof-of-life videos begging Obama to agree to a prisoner release in exchange for his freedom.

It took the CIA several weeks to confirm that the two hostages had indeed been killed in the strike, at which point the agency notified President Obama, who then called the families and personally apologized for their deaths. Obama hadn't ordered the drone strike, however. In fact, he didn't even know about it at the time. As it turns out, Pakistan is the only country where an anonymous CIA official, rather than the president of the United States, can authorize a "signature" drone strike against a specific target, without knowing if any specific, presumably "high-value" terrorist suspects are actually present there.

The deaths of the two Western hostages succeeded in doing what the killing of thousands of innocent Pakistanis, Afghanis, and Yemenis in US drone strikes had failed to accomplish. It provoked the *New York Times*, frustrated with the lack of congressional oversight over the drone program, to defy the CIA and publish the name of the man, who as head of the agency's Counterterrorism Center (CTC), was a key "architect of the targeted killing program." His name is Michael D'Andrea, and *Times* reporter Mark Mazzetti described him as "a gaunt, chain-smoking convert to Islam."

By the time Mazzetti outed D'Andrea in April 2015, however, he was no longer drone assassination chief, after being forced out of the agency following the disastrous Shawal Valley strike. It turned out that, among national security reporters like Mazzetti, D'Andrea's identity and central role within both the agency's torture and targeted killing programs had been an open secret for years. But he was always identified in various newspaper articles and books only by his first name, "Mike," or his undercover alias, "Roger."

Before Mazzetti outed him in the *Times*, the most in-depth article about D'Andrea was written in 2012 by *Washington Post* national security reporter Greg Miller. "For every cloud of smoke that follows a CIA drone strike in Pakistan, dozens of smaller plumes can be traced to a gaunt figure standing in a courtyard near the center of the agency's Langley campus in Virginia," Miller wrote. "He presides over a campaign that has killed thousands of Islamist militants and angered millions of Muslims, but he is himself a convert to Islam."

Within the CIA, Michael D'Andrea was viewed as a competitive workaholic who had somehow managed to survive several tedious years in the agency's clandestine service in Africa (during which time he married a Muslim woman and converted to Islam) before being assigned managerial status. Rising through the ranks of the clandestine service, he operated in Egypt and Iraq, among other locations.

By the time of the Shawal Valley strike, D'Andrea already was a controversial figure in intelligence circles. He was one of the agency officials who failed to keep track of Nawaf Al-Hamzi, one of the 9/11 hijackers, after he entered the United States.

As revealed by *New Yorker* magazine reporter Jane Mayer in her book *The Dark Side*, a chronicle of the US government's post-9/11 descent into torture and other criminality, the CIA knew that Al-Hamzi was in the United States. An FBI officer named Doug Miller who was attached to the CIA typed up a memo about Hamzi, hoping to share the tip with the FBI so they could locate the suspected terrorist. "But his boss, a CIA desk officer in the bin Laden unit of the Counterterrorist Center who is identified by the 9/11 commission only as 'Mike' told Miller to hold off on sending the memo," Mayer wrote. "After the second try, Miller dropped the matter." Three hours after "Mike" gave that order, he inexplicably told his CIA superiors that the tip had, in fact, been passed to the FBI. "The CIA assumed from then on that it was," adds Mayer. "But it wasn't."

"Mike" was Michael D'Andrea. While researching her book, Mayer spoke with a 9/11 Commission investigator, who told her that under questioning, D'Andrea conveniently couldn't remember anything about the Al-Hamzi episode. "Astonishingly," Mayer wrote in her book, "the 9/11 investigator later learned [that D'Andrea] was given a promotion by the agency after September 11."

D'Andrea also supervised an operation that resulted in one of the costliest miscalculations in America's war on terror when a doctor in Jordan named Humam Balawi convinced Jordanian intelligence, and then the CIA, that he could infiltrate al-Qaeda's top leadership. "The CIA at the highest levels, especially 'Mike,' was so excited by the possibility of finally having an agent inside the terrorist group, that the news was hurried all the way to the Oval Office," reported the veteran British-born national security correspondent Andrew Cockburn in his 2015 book *Kill Chain*. But Balawi had no intention of helping the CIA. Instead, on December 30, 2009, he wore an explosive vest to an introductory meeting at an agency station in Khost, Afghanistan, where he was welcomed by several CIA officers including the base's commander Jennifer Matthews, a veteran of the CTC who had spent years trying to track down bin Laden. Seven CIA employees, including Matthews, perished when Balawi blew himself up.

D'Andrea was the driving force behind the sharp escalation of the drone killing program in Pakistan, with the number of missions jumping from just three in 2006 to 117 in 2010—a pace of roughly one every three days. He also argued for the implementation of "signature" strikes where, as in the case of the botched Shawal Valley raid, the CIA could blow up a building simply because its inhabitants seemed suspicious.

With his growing reputation as a fire-breathing terrorist hunter, it is not surprising that the CIA talked up his story to the *Zero Dark Thirty* filmmakers. In the movie, D'Andrea became the inspiration for a character named "The Wolf," an enigmatic CIA supervisor in charge of the Alec Station, the CIA's bin Laden–tracking unit, which was essentially a high-tech, anti-terrorist death squad. "People were scared of [D'Andrea]," one former US intelligence official told Miller of the *Washington Post*. "[He] was the undertaker."

* * *

The Shawal disaster appears to have been D'Andrea's undoing. In March 2015, a month before news of the errant missile killing two hostages reached the public, Miller reported that D'Andrea was quietly being removed from his job as director of the CIA's Counterterrorism Center. His responsibility for the Khost suicide bombing fiasco as well as his deep involvement in the CIA's torture program had left him "tainted." The Shawal disaster was the final nail in his CIA career.

Why did it take so long for an intelligence official with a track record as notorious as D'Andrea's to be reported on by name in the press? It was only after he had antagonized the Obama White House by exposing the drone program to wide criticism following the Shawal disaster, and official Washington had thrown him under the bus, that the *New York Times* and other media outlets felt safe enough to identify "the undertaker."

Mark Mazzetti, the *Times* reporter who finally exposed D'Andrea's identity, had always tried to play by the rules of the national security beat. So while he had mentioned D'Andrea in *The Way of the Knife*, his 2014 book about the CIA's counter-terror operations in the Middle East and South Asia, Mazzetti was careful to only use his first name. "He was someone we had known about for a long time," recalled the reporter.

As D'Andrea climbed the ranks at the CIA, with controversy swirling around him, Mazzetti concluded it was legitimate to name him. "Everyone who covers this beat knows the names of dozens of undercover officers, but for me, there were personally two factors in naming him. These guys are in senior management jobs that give them oversight over hundreds or thousands of people. They are not guys in the field out there undercover working sources."

The CIA pushed back. According to Mazzetti, CIA Director John Brennan telephoned *Times* editor Dean Baquet, hoping to convince Baquet to quash the D'Andrea story. "I think you can judge seriousness by how high they escalate it," Mazzetti observed. "When it gets to the [CIA] director calling our executive editor, it shows they are taking it seriously."

Mazzetti thought that in D'Andrea's case, the CIA's argument was absurd. "At that level in the CIA, you're a public figure. It's bullshit to be undercover; you represent the agency at that stage. These guys are the modern generals running a secret war. This is how America goes to war now, and these are the generals running it."

After the Shawal disaster, the *Times* found the CIA's argument unpersuasive and the infamous counter-terrorism chief was suddenly dragged from the shadows. By playing by the CIA's rules for years, however, the Washington media had allowed D'Andrea—a dangerously kill-happy and flagrantly incompetent administrator—to keep rising through the intelligence ranks. Despite his increasingly tainted reputation within the agency, none of the press watchdogs dared to mention D'Andrea by name until Langley had already thrown him overboard.

Mark Mazzetti, like the rest of Washington's small club of national security reporters who are given access at Langley, must constantly engage in the intricate choreography that accompanies his beat. In this dance with security officials, reporters sometimes take the lead, but usually can only respond to Langley's initiatives.

In December 2007, Mazzetti informed the CIA that he was about to publish a story revealing that Jose Rodriguez, the agency's clandestine service chief, had destroyed evidence concerning the torture of two terrorist suspects, Abu Zubaydah, a reputed intimate of bin Laden and one of the first al-Qaeda suspects captured in Pakistan, and Abd al-Rahim al-Nashiri, alleged mastermind of the bombing of the USS Cole. "I went to the CIA and told them I was going to write the story," Mazzetti recalled. "I told them I was going to write it in two days, and put it in Friday's paper. On Thursday, they called and said, 'Are you really going to do this story?'"

After Mazzetti responded in the affirmative, an agency spokesperson informed him that then-CIA Director Michael Hayden had just informed his staff that the destruction of the tapes was about to be made public. Suddenly, the *Times* reporter found himself scooped by Langley with apparent advance notice given to the Associated Press, presumably to punish him for trying to outsmart the CIA, while rewarding a rival reporter viewed as more friendly to the agency.

"That's one of the risks we run when we have stories not favorable to the administration or CIA or Pentagon," said Jonathan Landay of McClatchy Newspapers. "If we give them too much time, they will leak their version to someone else and upstage you. We are very cautious about when we inform a government agency that we are writing a story that they might not like, because we are very concerned they might leak a more positive version to a competitor. We can't give them too much time to respond, because they will leak it to someone else."

Mazzetti compared the CIA to "a big public high school" with "so many cliques and agendas and factions that when you are talking to someone it is hard to know which faction they are from and what axes they have to grind. So you have to treat [everything] with caution," he said, estimating that reporters are lucky if they know even 20 percent of the facts behind a particular story. "That's a disadvantage for a journalist, but twenty percent is critically important if your job is to let people know about what's going on in secret."

* * *

Knowing what is going on in secret is, of course, the primary directive of all national security reporters. But trying to gain access to such secrets puts the scoop-hungry Washington press corps in a position of perpetual subordination and supplication in relation to covert government agencies. Reporters offend their official sources at their peril, for they will soon find themselves out of the loop, cut off from the morsels of leaked intelligence that are these beat journalists' daily bread and butter.

This is what it all comes down to: the CIA no longer needs to recruit media reporters and put them on its payroll. Instead, the agency simply relies on a finely tuned set of relationships with a select group of elite reporters who are utterly dependent on the national security state for their professional survival.

One of those elite reporters is James Risen of the *New York Times*. He is among the few who sometimes bites the hand that feeds him. Risen, working with fellow *Times* reporter Eric Lichtblau, authored one of the most important national security exposés since 9/11, uncovering the existence of "Stellar Wind," a warrantless wiretapping operation aimed at American citizens authorized by President George W. Bush and carried out by the National Security Agency (NSA) without the consent or knowledge of Congress. But aggressive reporting is not enough in the national security world, where bold reporters need equally bold editors. Unfortunately, Risen and Lichtblau had the *Times*' Washington bureau chief, Philip Taubman, and executive editors Howell Raines and then Bill Keller—the two top editors who presided over the WMD and Judith Miller fiasco.

The Stellar Wind exposé was due to run just before the 2004 presidential election. But under strong pressure from Bush national security advisor Condoleezza Rice and NSA chief Michael Hayden, who took the unusual step of inviting Taubman to NSA headquarters at Fort Meade, Maryland, the *Times* editors sat on the Stellar Wind scoop for over a year. The Bush team's lobbying campaign worked. As Taubman later recalled, so it reads As Taubman later recalled, "The administration persuaded Bill and me at the time that we literally might be putting American lives in danger. . . . There was a growing sense that the Bush administration might be contravening the law, but we were persuaded after meeting with Condoleezza Rice and Hayden that it was critical to preventing terrorism."

In his recent memoir, Hayden praised the compliant Taubman as "responsible" and "balanced," accolades that Taubman "may never live down," as national security reporter Mark Bowden wryly remarked in his *Times* review of the book.

In the end, the *New York Times* only ran the story in December 2005 after Risen forced the hand of his editors by threatening to scoop his own newspaper and break the Stellar Wind story in his book, *State of War: The Secret History of the CIA and the Bush Administration*, which was scheduled to be published the following month. "They were furious. They thought I was being insubordinate, which I was," Risen later told *Vanity Fair*.

Even to the very end, the administration tried to scare the *Times* into spiking the story, with President Bush himself summoning Taubman, Keller, and publisher Arthur Ochs Sulzberger Jr. to the Oval Office for one final round of fear mongering, where Bush warned of another 9/11 attack if the Stellar Wind exposé ran. This time, the *Times* refused to cave, the story was published, and of course "the sky did not fall," as noted by Bowden.

In the end, the spooking of the news works, because the news media allows it to work. The strongest deterrent to independent reporting is not the CIA or NSA, but the relentless will of the corporate media to conform to official government policy.

"By and large, I think the tendency of the media to conform to government doctrine and corporate needs is much more deeply rooted than anything involving the CIA," argues Noam Chomsky, the famed linguist and power critic.

"The CIA nowadays doesn't really have to buy journalists," agreed radical scholar Peter Dale Scott, author of *The American Deep State*. "Journalists step into line voluntarily to be eligible for promotion and have good relations inside the government, and they are selected for promotion based on their willingness to accept government lies." Scott experienced the same phenomenon decades ago when he briefly served as a bureaucrat in Canada's foreign service. "You either play the game or think for yourself. There is an updraft at the center of the system that is equivalent to buying people off. People are selected for promotion by their willingness to accept government lies. Gary Webb challenged the lies and he's dead."

Through most of his career, Gary Webb was a gung-ho believer in the free press, the way it's taught in journalism schools. But after he was roughed up and driven out of the profession that he loved at the hands of CIA-friendly media gatekeepers, Webb saw his sad tale as an important warning for all investigative journalists. "I was winning awards, getting raises, lecturing college classes, appearing on TV shows, and judging journalism contests," he recalled before his death. "And then I wrote some stories that made me realize how sadly misplaced my bliss had been. The reason I'd enjoyed such smooth sailing for so long hadn't been, as I'd assumed, because I was careful and diligent and good at my job. . . . The truth was that, in all those years, I hadn't written anything important enough to suppress."

Time and time again, America's most powerful news institutions have protected government institutions engaged in illegal behavior that undermine American society's most deeply cherished democratic values. The interests of the national security state and those of a robust and independent press always have been and always will be diametrically opposed. This oppositional notion is, of course, the founding principle of a free press. Yet sadly, as this book has revealed, it is much more myth than reality. Our leading media institutions have sold out to the powerful, covert agencies they should be holding accountable. So long as these shadowy institutions continue to operate with nearly unchecked power, secrecy will remain their most potent weapon. The spooking of the news will continue and the struggle against it—more lopsided yet more crucial than ever before—will be won or lost one story at a time.

Author's
Acknowledgments

T his book was the brilliant idea of my editor, David Talbot. It would not have been possible without the generous cooperation of my sources: national security journalists, former intelligence officers, academic scholars and historical researchers. Special thanks goes to Robert Baer, Bryan Bender, Noam Chomsky, Adam Goldman, John Kiriakou, Peter Kornbluh, Jason Leopold, Mark Mazzetti, Bob Parry, James Risen, Peter Dale Scott, Frank Snepp, and Jeff Stein. I also owe a debt of gratitude to Mary Alexander and Norman Schou for reading early drafts of the book and to Gustavo Arellano, editor-in-chief at *OC Weekly*, for not firing me while I wrote it. As always, love and appreciation to my wife and son, Claudia and Erik Schou, for their moral support and eternal patience.

Nicholas Schou, March 2016.

Endnotes

Chapter One

1   "I eat pretty much anything": Maas, Peter. "Are You There CIA?
     It's Me, Siobhan," *The Intercept*, Dec. 2 2014.

2   "the masked executioner was actually a Kuwaiti-born British
     national": Goldman, Adam. "'Jihadi John': Islamic State Killer is
     Identified as Londoner Mohammed Emwazi," *Washington Post*,
     February 26, 2015.

3   "personally approved by George Bush": Stein, Jeff. "How the
     CIA Took Down Hezbollah's Top Terrorist, Imad Mugniyah,"
     Newsweek, January 31, 2015.

4   "internal CIA practice known as an 'eyewash'": "Miller, Greg
     and Goldman, Adam. "Eyewash: How the CIA Deceives its
     Own Workforce About Operations, *Washington Post*, Jan. 31,
     2016.

5   "the importance of the story justifies publication": Calderone,
     Michael. "*New York Times* Withheld News of Missing American's
     CIA Ties for Six Years," *The Huffington Post*, Dec. 13, 2013.

6   "Levinson, who remains missing, holds that record": On Jan. 21, 2016, the *New York Times* published a story based on secret cables allegedly showing that Iran is still holding Levinson prisoner.

Chapter Two

7   "were enough to rock the Fourth Estate": Bernstein, Carl. "The CIA and the Media: How America's Most Powerful News Media Worked Hand in Glove with the Central Intelligence Agency and Why the Church Committee Covered it Up," *Rolling Stone*, Oct. 20, 1977.

8   "Thank you for your kind and informative letter": As indicated, all quotes from this exchange come from the CIA's Family Jewels file: www.foia.cia.gov/collection/family-jewels

9   "There would be no place left to hide.": "The Intelligence Gathering Debate," *Meet the Press*, NBC, Aug. 17, 1975.

10 "with responses that were often, in fact, quite untrue": Chamorro, Edgar. *Packaging the Contras: A Case of CIA Disinformation,* Institute for Media Analysis, Inc. Monograph Series #2, 1987. p. 11.

11 "'regional Soviet interests,' 'foreign agents,' and 'totalitarian.' Ibid, p. 17.

12 "distancing Nicaraguans from their rightful Bishops": Riding, Alan. "Pope Says Taking Sides In Nicaragua Is Peril To Church," *New York Times*, March 5, 1983.

13 "We tried to get stories published in the European press": Chamorro, p. 22.

14 "Nicaraguan side of the border": Ibid, p. 32.

15 "hero of the contras had been executed": Ibid, p. 35.

16 "Everyone always says more than they're supposed to": Woodward, Bob. *Veil: The Secret Wars of the CIA 1981-1987,* Simon & Schuster, p. 14.

17 "Concerns Grow on Soviet Plans in Poland": Ibid, p. 66.

18 "It could be bad": Ibid, p. 190.

19 "Oliver North's covert and illegal funding of the contras": Parry, Robert and Barger, Brian. "Reports Link Nicaraguan Rebels to Cocaine Trafficking," AP Wire, Dec. 20, 1985.

20   "that finally exposed the machinations of the Office of Public
       Diplomacy": Kornbluh, Peter, and Parry, Robert. "Iran-Contra's
       Untold Story," *Foreign Policy*, Autumn, 1988.

Chapter Three

21   "with his most reliable supply of cheap cocaine": See Webb, Gary.
       *Dark Alliance: The CIA, The Contras, and the Crack Cocaine
       Explosion*, Seven Stories Press, 1998.

22   "the reinstatement of democracy in Nicaragua": Webb, Gary.
       "Dark Alliance: Day One." *San Jose Mercury News*, Aug. 8, 1996.

23   "the ends justify the means": Webb, p. 73.

24   "his friends in Washington weren't going to like what was going
       on": Webb, p. 324.

25   "how his colleagues would go after him": Schou, Nick. *Kill the
       Messenger: How the CIA's Crack Cocaine Epidemic Destroyed
       Journalist Gary Webb*, Nation Books, 2006, p. 75.

26   "You're the TV man": Cockburn, Alexander and St. Clair, Jeffrey,
       White Out: The CIA, Drugs & the Press, Verso, 1999, p. 31.

27   "portrayed his Latin American arms deals as the work of a
       bumbling imposter": Merina, Victor and Rempel, William C.
       "Ex-Associates Doubt One-Time Drug Trafficker's Claim of CIA
       Ties," *Los Angeles Times*, Oct. 21, 1996.

28   "either not new, not significant, or not supported by real evi-
       dence": Schou, p. 135.

29   "college weekend with the Russians": Wilford, Hugh. "*The Mighty
       Wurlitzer: How the CIA Played America*," Harvard University
       Press, 2008, p. 146.

30   "That might have helped me understand what was going on
       there a bit": Grim, Ryan. "Kill the Messenger: How the Media
       Destroyed Gary Webb," *The Huffington Post*, Oct. 10, 2014.

31   "dismissed him as the author of 'discredited' work": Lelyveld, Nita
       and Hymon, Steve. "Gary Webb, 49, Wrote Series Linking CIA,
       Drugs," *Los Angeles Times*, Dec. 12, 2004.

32   "by talking 'one major news affiliate' out of covering the story":
       "Managing a Nightmare: CIA Public Affairs and the Drug
       Conspiracy Story," *Studies in Intelligence*, 1997.

33   "This success has to be seen in relative terms": Devereaux, Ryan. "Managing a Nightmare: How the CIA Oversaw the Destruction of Gary Webb, *The Intercept*, Sept. 25, 2014.

34   "concerning an exiled Saudi Arabian "dissident" named Osama bin Laden": Wright, Robin. "Saudi Dissident a Prime Suspect in Blasts," *Los Angeles Times*, Aug. 14, 1998.

Chapter Four

35   "We are inevitably the mouthpiece for whatever administration is in power": Mitchell, Greg. *So Wrong for So Long: How the Press, the Pundits—and the President—Failed on Iraq*. Union Square Press. 2008, p. 2.

36   "opposing viewpoints simply got lost": Ibid. p. 4.

37   "to store radiological and other unconventional weapons": Miller, Judith. *The Story: A Reporter's Journey*. Simon & Schuster, 2015. p. 154.

38   "underground wells, private villas and under the Saddam Hussein Hospital": Miller, Judith. "An Iraqi Defector Tells of Work on at Least 20 Hidden Weapons Sites," *New York Times*, Dec. 20, 2001.

39   "failed to find evidence": Wemple, Eric. "Judith Miller Tries, and Ultimately Fails, to Defend Her Flawed Iraq Reporting," *Washington Post*, April 9, 2015.

40   "part of his campaign against the West": Miller, Judith and Gordon, Michael "Threats and Responses: The Iraqis; U.S. Says Hussein Intensifies Quest for A-Bomb Parts," *New York Times*, Sept. 8, 2002.

41   "But we don't want the smoking gun to be a mushroom cloud": Blitzer, Wolf. "Search For the Smoking Gun," CNN, Jan. 10, 2003.

42   "overwrought and misinformed": Miller, Greg, "When the 'NYT' Offered a Weak 'Mini-Culpa' for Hyping Iraq WMD," *The Nation*, March 15, 2013.

43   "defectors provided by Chalabi": Miller, Judith, *The Story*, p. 207.

44   "one of the low points": Ibid, p. 318.

45   "finally demolishing it in a May 5, 2002 story": Isikoff, Michael. "The Phantom Link to Iraq." *Newsweek*, May 5, 2002.

46   "There's just too much there": Mitchell, p. 25.

47   "only a fool—or possibly a Frenchman": Ibid, p. 26.

48   "almost no pictures from Iraq of Americans killed in action": Ibid, p. 123.

49   "undermining U.S. credibility in Iraq": Landay, Jonathan S. "U.S. Military Pays Iraqis for Positive News Stories," *Knight Ridder*, Nov. 30, 2005.

50   "Because publishers must be free to publish": *60 Minutes*, Jan. 30, 2011.

51   "had worked with British intelligence": Greenwald, Glenn and Gallagher, Ryan, "Snowden Documents Reveal Covert Surveillance and Pressure Tactics Aimed at WikiLeaks and its Supporters, *The Intercept*, Feb. 17, 2014.

52   "muddled, incoherent, often inconsequential mess": Greenwald, Glenn. *No Place to Hide: Edward Snowden, The NSA, and the U.S. Surveillance State*. Metropolitan Books, 2014, p. 56.

Chapter Five

53   "they look all right": Koppel, Ted and Montaigne, Rene. "Visiting the Prison at Guantanamo Bay," NPR, July 14, 2006.

54   "a cozy forum to talk about terrorism": Wasserman, Edward. "Ted Koppel Offers Officials a Cozy Forum on Terrorism," *New York Times*, Sept. 9, 2006.

55   "died while under torture, accidentally or intentionally": Horton, Scott. "The Guantanamo 'Suicides': A Camp Delta Sergeant Blows the Whistle," *Harper's Magazine*, March, 2010.

56   "after becoming suspicious about the deaths of inmates at Guantanamo": Leopold, Jason and Kaye, Jeffrey. "Exclusive: Controversial Drug Given to All Guantanamo Detainees Akin to Pharmacologic Waterboarding, *Truthout*, Dec. 1, 2010.

57   "came under vitriolic attack": Hickman, Joseph. *Murder at Camp Delta: A Staff Sergeant's Pursuit of the Truth About Guantanamo Bay*, Simon and Schuster, 2015.

Chapter Six

58   "flipping the good- and bad-guy roles": Alford, Matthew and Graham, Robbie. "Body of Lies: The CIA's Involvement with U.S. Film-making." *The Guardian*, Nov. 13, 2008.

59   "a propaganda film for America": Ibid.
60   "a former Navy counterinsurgency specialist": Butterfield, Fox.
      "Washington Talk; Contra Connection; Stalking Film Rights,"
      New York Times, Jan. 29, 1987.
61   "We've always been portrayed as evil and Machiavellian":
      Patterson, John. "The Caring, Sharing CIA: Central Intelligence
      Gets a Makeover." *The Guardian*. Oct. 4, 2001.
62   "Brandon was on set to advise": Alford and Graham, *The
      Guardian*.
63   "Mrs. Garner was excited to participate in the video": "New
      Recruitment Video on the CIA Careers Site," CIA press release,
      March 8, 2004.
64   "such a storyline would embarrass the CIA": Patterson, *The
      Guardian*.
65   "a creepy publicity stunt staged by the *New York Times*: Galanes,
      Philip, "Homeland Times Two: Clair Danes and Jeh Johnson,"
      New York Times, Oct. 17, 2015.
66   "and shared other classified information with the filmmakers":
      Harris, Shane. "Panetta Revealed Top Secret Information to
      Filmmaker," *Washingtonian*, May 21, 2013.
67   "the report cleared them of any wrongdoing": Leopold, Jason.
      "Tequila, Painted Pearls, and Prada-How the CIA Helped
      Produce *Zero Dark Thirty*." *Vice*, Sept. 15, 2015.
68   "there was no climactic firefight": Cummings, Michael and Eric.
      "How Accurate is *Lone Survivor*?" *Slate*, Jan. 10, 2014.
69   "It would take an article longer than this one": Leen, Jeff.
      "Gary Webb Was No Journalism Hero, Despite What 'Kill the
      Messenger' Says, *Washington Post*, Oct. 17, 2014.

Chapter Seven

70   "might have been written by Lewis Carroll": Hersh, Seymour.
      "The Killing of Osama bin Laden," *London Review of Books*, May
      2015.
71   "There's always one guy who tells you the secret": Wemple, Erik,
      "Sy Hersh: I Could Go On and On About the Press," *Washington
      Post*, May 11, 2015.

72   "a farrago of nonsense": Lamothe, Dan. "Utter Nonsense: CIA and White House Blast Seymour Hersh's Explosive Osama bin Laden Raid Story," *Washington Post*, May 11, 2015.

73   "inexplicably offered to let him write it as a blog": Farhi, Paul. "The Ever-Iconoclastic, Never-to-be-Ignored, Muckraking Seymour Hersh," *Washington Post*, May 15, 2015.

74   "directly contradicted the magazine's previous reporting": Sherman, Gabriel. "*Why Hersh's 'Alternative' bin Laden History Did Not Appear in the* New Yorker," *New York*, May 11, 2015.

75   "if only somebody can tell me precisely where he is": Shafer, Jack. "Sy Hersh, Lost in a Wilderness of Mirrors," *Politico*, May 11, 2015.

76   "It was going to be extremely difficult to corroborate it": Gall, Carlotta. "The Detail in Seymour Hersh's Bin Laden Story That Rings True," *New York Times*, May 12, 2015.

Conclusion

77   "possibly members of the Islamic Movement of Uzbekistan": Mazzetti, Mark and Schmitt, Eric. "First Evidence of a Blunder in Drone Strike: Two Extra Bodies," *New York Times*, April 23, 2015.

78   "It provoked the *New York Times*": "Deep Support in Washington For CIA's Drone Mission," by Mark Mazzetti and Matt Apuzzo, *New York Times*, April 25, 2015.

79   "For every cloud of smoke": "At CIA, a Convert to Islam Leads the Terrorism Hunt," by Greg Miller, *The Washington Post*, March 24, 2012.

80   "the 9/11 investigator later learned": Mayer, Jane. *The Dark Side: The Inside Story of How the War on Terror Turned Into a War on American Ideals*, Random House, 2008, p. 16.

81   "the news was hurried all the way to the Oval Office": Cockburn, Andrew. *Kill Chain: The Rise of the High-Tech Assassins*, Henry Holt & Co., March 2015, p. 229.

82   "D'Andrea was quietly being removed from his office": Miller, Greg. "CIA Official Who Led the Hunt for Bin Laden is Being Removed From Post," *Washington Post*, March 25, 2015.

83   "a rival reporter viewed as more friendly to the agency": Mazzetti, Mark. "CIA Destroyed Two Tapes Showing Interrogations," *New York Times*, Dec. 7, 2007.

84   "Stellar Wind,' a warrantless wiretapping operation": Risen, James, and Lichtblau, Eric. "Bush Lets U.S. Spy on Callers Without Courts," *New York Times*, Dec. 15, 2005.

85   "I hadn't written anything important enough to supress": Borjesson, Kristina (Edited by). *Into the Buzzsaw: Leading Journalists Expose the Myth of a Free Press,* Prometheus Books, 2002. p. 156.